C-4212   CAREER EXAMINATION SERIES

This is your
PASSBOOK for...

Psychiatric Technician

Test Preparation Study Guide
Questions & Answers

COPYRIGHT NOTICE

This book is SOLELY intended for, is sold ONLY to, and its use is RESTRICTED to individual, bona fide applicants or candidates who qualify by virtue of having seriously filed applications for appropriate license, certificate, professional and/or promotional advancement, higher school matriculation, scholarship, or other legitimate requirements of education and/or governmental authorities.

This book is NOT intended for use, class instruction, tutoring, training, duplication, copying, reprinting, excerption, or adaptation, etc., by:

1) Other publishers
2) Proprietors and/or Instructors of "Coaching" and/or Preparatory Courses
3) Personnel and/or Training Divisions of commercial, industrial, and governmental organizations
4) Schools, colleges, or universities and/or their departments and staffs, including teachers and other personnel
5) Testing Agencies or Bureaus
6) Study groups which seek by the purchase of a single volume to copy and/or duplicate and/or adapt this material for use by the group as a whole without having purchased individual volumes for each of the members of the group
7) Et al.

Such persons would be in violation of appropriate Federal and State statutes.

PROVISION OF LICENSING AGREEMENTS – Recognized educational, commercial, industrial, and governmental institutions and organizations, and others legitimately engaged in educational pursuits, including training, testing, and measurement activities, may address request for a licensing agreement to the copyright owners, who will determine whether, and under what conditions, including fees and charges, the materials in this book may be used them. In other words, a licensing facility exists for the legitimate use of the material in this book on other than an individual basis. However, it is asseverated and affirmed here that the material in this book CANNOT be used without the receipt of the express permission of such a licensing agreement from the Publishers. Inquiries re licensing should be addressed to the company, attention rights and permissions department.

All rights reserved, including the right of reproduction in whole or in part, in any form or by any means, electronic or mechanical, including photocopying, recording, or by any information storage and retrieval system, without permission in writing from the Publisher.

Copyright © 2024 by
National Learning Corporation

212 Michael Drive, Syosset, NY 11791
(516) 921-8888 • www.passbooks.com
E-mail: info@passbooks.com

PUBLISHED IN THE UNITED STATES OF AMERICA

PASSBOOK® SERIES

THE *PASSBOOK® SERIES* has been created to prepare applicants and candidates for the ultimate academic battlefield – the examination room.

At some time in our lives, each and every one of us may be required to take an examination – for validation, matriculation, admission, qualification, registration, certification, or licensure.

Based on the assumption that every applicant or candidate has met the basic formal educational standards, has taken the required number of courses, and read the necessary texts, the *PASSBOOK® SERIES* furnishes the one special preparation which may assure passing with confidence, instead of failing with insecurity. Examination questions – together with answers – are furnished as the basic vehicle for study so that the mysteries of the examination and its compounding difficulties may be eliminated or diminished by a sure method.

This book is meant to help you pass your examination provided that you qualify and are serious in your objective.

The entire field is reviewed through the huge store of content information which is succinctly presented through a provocative and challenging approach – the question-and-answer method.

A climate of success is established by furnishing the correct answers at the end of each test.

You soon learn to recognize types of questions, forms of questions, and patterns of questioning. You may even begin to anticipate expected outcomes.

You perceive that many questions are repeated or adapted so that you can gain acute insights, which may enable you to score many sure points.

You learn how to confront new questions, or types of questions, and to attack them confidently and work out the correct answers.

You note objectives and emphases, and recognize pitfalls and dangers, so that you may make positive educational adjustments.

Moreover, you are kept fully informed in relation to new concepts, methods, practices, and directions in the field.

You discover that you are actually taking the examination all the time: you are preparing for the examination by "taking" an examination, not by reading extraneous and/or supererogatory textbooks.

In short, this PASSBOOK®, used directedly, should be an important factor in helping you to pass your test.

PSYCHIATRIC TECHNICIAN

An entry-level health care provider who is responsible for care of mentally disordered and developmentally disabled clients. A psychiatric technician practices under the direction of physician, psychologist, rehabilitation therapist, social worker, registered nurse or other professional personnel. The licensee is not an independent practitioner. While there is no national licensure examination for PTs, California and other states administer a year round examination   When a PT applicant is approved, a Notice of Eligibility and Candidate Handbook is mailed.

HOW TO TAKE A TEST

I. YOU MUST PASS AN EXAMINATION

A. *WHAT EVERY CANDIDATE SHOULD KNOW*

Examination applicants often ask us for help in preparing for the written test. What can I study in advance? What kinds of questions will be asked? How will the test be given? How will the papers be graded?

As an applicant for a civil service examination, you may be wondering about some of these things. Our purpose here is to suggest effective methods of advance study and to describe civil service examinations.

Your chances for success on this examination can be increased if you know how to prepare. Those "pre-examination jitters" can be reduced if you know what to expect. You can even experience an adventure in good citizenship if you know why civil service exams are given.

B. *WHY ARE CIVIL SERVICE EXAMINATIONS GIVEN?*

Civil service examinations are important to you in two ways. As a citizen, you want public jobs filled by employees who know how to do their work. As a job seeker, you want a fair chance to compete for that job on an equal footing with other candidates. The best-known means of accomplishing this two-fold goal is the competitive examination.

Exams are widely publicized throughout the nation. They may be administered for jobs in federal, state, city, municipal, town or village governments or agencies.

Any citizen may apply, with some limitations, such as the age or residence of applicants. Your experience and education may be reviewed to see whether you meet the requirements for the particular examination. When these requirements exist, they are reasonable and applied consistently to all applicants. Thus, a competitive examination may cause you some uneasiness now, but it is your privilege and safeguard.

C. *HOW ARE CIVIL SERVICE EXAMS DEVELOPED?*

Examinations are carefully written by trained technicians who are specialists in the field known as "psychological measurement," in consultation with recognized authorities in the field of work that the test will cover. These experts recommend the subject matter areas or skills to be tested; only those knowledges or skills important to your success on the job are included. The most reliable books and source materials available are used as references. Together, the experts and technicians judge the difficulty level of the questions.

Test technicians know how to phrase questions so that the problem is clearly stated. Their ethics do not permit "trick" or "catch" questions. Questions may have been tried out on sample groups, or subjected to statistical analysis, to determine their usefulness.

Written tests are often used in combination with performance tests, ratings of training and experience, and oral interviews. All of these measures combine to form the best-known means of finding the right person for the right job.

II. HOW TO PASS THE WRITTEN TEST

A. NATURE OF THE EXAMINATION

To prepare intelligently for civil service examinations, you should know how they differ from school examinations you have taken. In school you were assigned certain definite pages to read or subjects to cover. The examination questions were quite detailed and usually emphasized memory. Civil service exams, on the other hand, try to discover your present ability to perform the duties of a position, plus your potentiality to learn these duties. In other words, a civil service exam attempts to predict how successful you will be. Questions cover such a broad area that they cannot be as minute and detailed as school exam questions.

In the public service similar kinds of work, or positions, are grouped together in one "class." This process is known as *position-classification*. All the positions in a class are paid according to the salary range for that class. One class title covers all of these positions, and they are all tested by the same examination.

B. FOUR BASIC STEPS

1) Study the announcement

How, then, can you know what subjects to study? Our best answer is: "Learn as much as possible about the class of positions for which you've applied." The exam will test the knowledge, skills and abilities needed to do the work.

Your most valuable source of information about the position you want is the official exam announcement. This announcement lists the training and experience qualifications. Check these standards and apply only if you come reasonably close to meeting them.

The brief description of the position in the examination announcement offers some clues to the subjects which will be tested. Think about the job itself. Review the duties in your mind. Can you perform them, or are there some in which you are rusty? Fill in the blank spots in your preparation.

Many jurisdictions preview the written test in the exam announcement by including a section called "Knowledge and Abilities Required," "Scope of the Examination," or some similar heading. Here you will find out specifically what fields will be tested.

2) Review your own background

Once you learn in general what the position is all about, and what you need to know to do the work, ask yourself which subjects you already know fairly well and which need improvement. You may wonder whether to concentrate on improving your strong areas or on building some background in your fields of weakness. When the announcement has specified "some knowledge" or "considerable knowledge," or has used adjectives like "beginning principles of…" or "advanced … methods," you can get a clue as to the number and difficulty of questions to be asked in any given field. More questions, and hence broader coverage, would be included for those subjects which are more important in the work. Now weigh your strengths and weaknesses against the job requirements and prepare accordingly.

3) Determine the level of the position

Another way to tell how intensively you should prepare is to understand the level of the job for which you are applying. Is it the entering level? In other words, is this the position in which beginners in a field of work are hired? Or is it an intermediate or advanced level? Sometimes this is indicated by such words as "Junior" or "Senior" in the class title. Other jurisdictions use Roman numerals to designate the level – Clerk I, Clerk II, for example. The word "Supervisor" sometimes appears in the title. If the level is not indicated by the title, check the description of duties. Will you be working under very close supervision, or will you have responsibility for independent decisions in this work?

4) Choose appropriate study materials

Now that you know the subjects to be examined and the relative amount of each subject to be covered, you can choose suitable study materials. For beginning level jobs, or even advanced ones, if you have a pronounced weakness in some aspect of your training, read a modern, standard textbook in that field. Be sure it is up to date and has general coverage. Such books are normally available at your library, and the librarian will be glad to help you locate one. For entry-level positions, questions of appropriate difficulty are chosen -- neither highly advanced questions, nor those too simple. Such questions require careful thought but not advanced training.

If the position for which you are applying is technical or advanced, you will read more advanced, specialized material. If you are already familiar with the basic principles of your field, elementary textbooks would waste your time. Concentrate on advanced textbooks and technical periodicals. Think through the concepts and review difficult problems in your field.

These are all general sources. You can get more ideas on your own initiative, following these leads. For example, training manuals and publications of the government agency which employs workers in your field can be useful, particularly for technical and professional positions. A letter or visit to the government department involved may result in more specific study suggestions, and certainly will provide you with a more definite idea of the exact nature of the position you are seeking.

III. KINDS OF TESTS

Tests are used for purposes other than measuring knowledge and ability to perform specified duties. For some positions, it is equally important to test ability to make adjustments to new situations or to profit from training. In others, basic mental abilities not dependent on information are essential. Questions which test these things may not appear as pertinent to the duties of the position as those which test for knowledge and information. Yet they are often highly important parts of a fair examination. For very general questions, it is almost impossible to help you direct your study efforts. What we can do is to point out some of the more common of these general abilities needed in public service positions and describe some typical questions.

1) General information

Broad, general information has been found useful for predicting job success in some kinds of work. This is tested in a variety of ways, from vocabulary lists to questions about current events. Basic background in some field of work, such as sociology or economics, may be sampled in a group of questions. Often these are principles which have become familiar to most persons through exposure rather than through formal training. It is difficult to advise you how to study for these questions; being alert to the world around you is our best suggestion.

2) Verbal ability

An example of an ability needed in many positions is verbal or language ability. Verbal ability is, in brief, the ability to use and understand words. Vocabulary and grammar tests are typical measures of this ability. Reading comprehension or paragraph interpretation questions are common in many kinds of civil service tests. You are given a paragraph of written material and asked to find its central meaning.

3) Numerical ability

Number skills can be tested by the familiar arithmetic problem, by checking paired lists of numbers to see which are alike and which are different, or by interpreting charts and graphs. In the latter test, a graph may be printed in the test booklet which you are asked to use as the basis for answering questions.

4) Observation

A popular test for law-enforcement positions is the observation test. A picture is shown to you for several minutes, then taken away. Questions about the picture test your ability to observe both details and larger elements.

5) Following directions

In many positions in the public service, the employee must be able to carry out written instructions dependably and accurately. You may be given a chart with several columns, each column listing a variety of information. The questions require you to carry out directions involving the information given in the chart.

6) Skills and aptitudes

Performance tests effectively measure some manual skills and aptitudes. When the skill is one in which you are trained, such as typing or shorthand, you can practice. These tests are often very much like those given in business school or high school courses. For many of the other skills and aptitudes, however, no short-time preparation can be made. Skills and abilities natural to you or that you have developed throughout your lifetime are being tested.

Many of the general questions just described provide all the data needed to answer the questions and ask you to use your reasoning ability to find the answers. Your best preparation for these tests, as well as for tests of facts and ideas, is to be at your physical and mental best. You, no doubt, have your own methods of getting into an exam-taking mood and keeping "in shape." The next section lists some ideas on this subject.

IV. KINDS OF QUESTIONS

Only rarely is the "essay" question, which you answer in narrative form, used in civil service tests. Civil service tests are usually of the short-answer type. Full instructions for answering these questions will be given to you at the examination. But in case this is your first experience with short-answer questions and separate answer sheets, here is what you need to know:

1) Multiple-choice Questions

Most popular of the short-answer questions is the "multiple choice" or "best answer" question. It can be used, for example, to test for factual knowledge, ability to solve problems or judgment in meeting situations found at work.

A multiple-choice question is normally one of three types—
- It can begin with an incomplete statement followed by several possible endings. You are to find the one ending which *best* completes the statement, although some of the others may not be entirely wrong.
- It can also be a complete statement in the form of a question which is answered by choosing one of the statements listed.

- It can be in the form of a problem – again you select the best answer.

Here is an example of a multiple-choice question with a discussion which should give you some clues as to the method for choosing the right answer:

When an employee has a complaint about his assignment, the action which will *best* help him overcome his difficulty is to
- A. discuss his difficulty with his coworkers
- B. take the problem to the head of the organization
- C. take the problem to the person who gave him the assignment
- D. say nothing to anyone about his complaint

In answering this question, you should study each of the choices to find which is best. Consider choice "A" – Certainly an employee may discuss his complaint with fellow employees, but no change or improvement can result, and the complaint remains unresolved. Choice "B" is a poor choice since the head of the organization probably does not know what assignment you have been given, and taking your problem to him is known as "going over the head" of the supervisor. The supervisor, or person who made the assignment, is the person who can clarify it or correct any injustice. Choice "C" is, therefore, correct. To say nothing, as in choice "D," is unwise. Supervisors have and interest in knowing the problems employees are facing, and the employee is seeking a solution to his problem.

2) True/False Questions

The "true/false" or "right/wrong" form of question is sometimes used. Here a complete statement is given. Your job is to decide whether the statement is right or wrong.

SAMPLE: A roaming cell-phone call to a nearby city costs less than a non-roaming call to a distant city.

This statement is wrong, or false, since roaming calls are more expensive.

This is not a complete list of all possible question forms, although most of the others are variations of these common types. You will always get complete directions for answering questions. Be sure you understand *how* to mark your answers – ask questions until you do.

V. RECORDING YOUR ANSWERS

Computer terminals are used more and more today for many different kinds of exams.
For an examination with very few applicants, you may be told to record your answers in the test booklet itself. Separate answer sheets are much more common. If this separate answer sheet is to be scored by machine – and this is often the case – it is highly important that you mark your answers correctly in order to get credit.
An electronic scoring machine is often used in civil service offices because of the speed with which papers can be scored. Machine-scored answer sheets must be marked with a pencil, which will be given to you. This pencil has a high graphite content which responds to the electronic scoring machine. As a matter of fact, stray dots may register as answers, so do not let your pencil rest on the answer sheet while you are pondering the correct answer. Also, if your pencil lead breaks or is otherwise defective, ask for another.

Since the answer sheet will be dropped in a slot in the scoring machine, be careful not to bend the corners or get the paper crumpled.

The answer sheet normally has five vertical columns of numbers, with 30 numbers to a column. These numbers correspond to the question numbers in your test booklet. After each number, going across the page are four or five pairs of dotted lines. These short dotted lines have small letters or numbers above them. The first two pairs may also have a "T" or "F" above the letters. This indicates that the first two pairs only are to be used if the questions are of the true-false type. If the questions are multiple choice, disregard the "T" and "F" and pay attention only to the small letters or numbers.

Answer your questions in the manner of the sample that follows:

32. The largest city in the United States is
    A. Washington, D.C.
    B. New York City
    C. Chicago
    D. Detroit
    E. San Francisco

1) Choose the answer you think is best. (New York City is the largest, so "B" is correct.)
2) Find the row of dotted lines numbered the same as the question you are answering. (Find row number 32)
3) Find the pair of dotted lines corresponding to the answer. (Find the pair of lines under the mark "B.")
4) Make a solid black mark between the dotted lines.

VI. BEFORE THE TEST

Common sense will help you find procedures to follow to get ready for an examination. Too many of us, however, overlook these sensible measures. Indeed, nervousness and fatigue have been found to be the most serious reasons why applicants fail to do their best on civil service tests. Here is a list of reminders:

- Begin your preparation early – Don't wait until the last minute to go scurrying around for books and materials or to find out what the position is all about.
- Prepare continuously – An hour a night for a week is better than an all-night cram session. This has been definitely established. What is more, a night a week for a month will return better dividends than crowding your study into a shorter period of time.
- Locate the place of the exam – You have been sent a notice telling you when and where to report for the examination. If the location is in a different town or otherwise unfamiliar to you, it would be well to inquire the best route and learn something about the building.
- Relax the night before the test – Allow your mind to rest. Do not study at all that night. Plan some mild recreation or diversion; then go to bed early and get a good night's sleep.
- Get up early enough to make a leisurely trip to the place for the test – This way unforeseen events, traffic snarls, unfamiliar buildings, etc. will not upset you.
- Dress comfortably – A written test is not a fashion show. You will be known by number and not by name, so wear something comfortable.

- Leave excess paraphernalia at home – Shopping bags and odd bundles will get in your way. You need bring only the items mentioned in the official notice you received; usually everything you need is provided. Do not bring reference books to the exam. They will only confuse those last minutes and be taken away from you when in the test room.
- Arrive somewhat ahead of time – If because of transportation schedules you must get there very early, bring a newspaper or magazine to take your mind off yourself while waiting.
- Locate the examination room – When you have found the proper room, you will be directed to the seat or part of the room where you will sit. Sometimes you are given a sheet of instructions to read while you are waiting. Do not fill out any forms until you are told to do so; just read them and be prepared.
- Relax and prepare to listen to the instructions
- If you have any physical problem that may keep you from doing your best, be sure to tell the test administrator. If you are sick or in poor health, you really cannot do your best on the exam. You can come back and take the test some other time.

VII. AT THE TEST

The day of the test is here and you have the test booklet in your hand. The temptation to get going is very strong. Caution! There is more to success than knowing the right answers. You must know how to identify your papers and understand variations in the type of short-answer question used in this particular examination. Follow these suggestions for maximum results from your efforts:

1) Cooperate with the monitor

The test administrator has a duty to create a situation in which you can be as much at ease as possible. He will give instructions, tell you when to begin, check to see that you are marking your answer sheet correctly, and so on. He is not there to guard you, although he will see that your competitors do not take unfair advantage. He wants to help you do your best.

2) Listen to all instructions

Don't jump the gun! Wait until you understand all directions. In most civil service tests you get more time than you need to answer the questions. So don't be in a hurry. Read each word of instructions until you clearly understand the meaning. Study the examples, listen to all announcements and follow directions. Ask questions if you do not understand what to do.

3) Identify your papers

Civil service exams are usually identified by number only. You will be assigned a number; you must not put your name on your test papers. Be sure to copy your number correctly. Since more than one exam may be given, copy your exact examination title.

4) Plan your time

Unless you are told that a test is a "speed" or "rate of work" test, speed itself is usually not important. Time enough to answer all the questions will be provided, but this does not mean that you have all day. An overall time limit has been set. Divide the total time (in minutes) by the number of questions to determine the approximate time you have for each question.

5) Do not linger over difficult questions

If you come across a difficult question, mark it with a paper clip (useful to have along) and come back to it when you have been through the booklet. One caution if you do this – be sure to skip a number on your answer sheet as well. Check often to be sure that you have not lost your place and that you are marking in the row numbered the same as the question you are answering.

6) Read the questions

Be sure you know what the question asks! Many capable people are unsuccessful because they failed to *read* the questions correctly.

7) Answer all questions

Unless you have been instructed that a penalty will be deducted for incorrect answers, it is better to guess than to omit a question.

8) Speed tests

It is often better NOT to guess on speed tests. It has been found that on timed tests people are tempted to spend the last few seconds before time is called in marking answers at random – without even reading them – in the hope of picking up a few extra points. To discourage this practice, the instructions may warn you that your score will be "corrected" for guessing. That is, a penalty will be applied. The incorrect answers will be deducted from the correct ones, or some other penalty formula will be used.

9) Review your answers

If you finish before time is called, go back to the questions you guessed or omitted to give them further thought. Review other answers if you have time.

10) Return your test materials

If you are ready to leave before others have finished or time is called, take ALL your materials to the monitor and leave quietly. Never take any test material with you. The monitor can discover whose papers are not complete, and taking a test booklet may be grounds for disqualification.

VIII. EXAMINATION TECHNIQUES

1) Read the general instructions carefully. These are usually printed on the first page of the exam booklet. As a rule, these instructions refer to the timing of the examination; the fact that you should not start work until the signal and must stop work at a signal, etc. If there are any *special* instructions, such as a choice of questions to be answered, make sure that you note this instruction carefully.

2) When you are ready to start work on the examination, that is as soon as the signal has been given, read the instructions to each question booklet, underline any key words or phrases, such as *least, best, outline, describe* and the like. In this way you will tend to answer as requested rather than discover on reviewing your paper that you *listed without describing*, that you selected the *worst* choice rather than the *best* choice, etc.

3) If the examination is of the objective or multiple-choice type – that is, each question will also give a series of possible answers: A, B, C or D, and you are called upon to select the best answer and write the letter next to that answer on your answer paper – it is advisable to start answering each question in turn. There may be anywhere from 50 to 100 such questions in the three or four hours allotted and you can see how much time would be taken if you read through all the questions before beginning to answer any. Furthermore, if you come across a question or group of questions which you know would be difficult to answer, it would undoubtedly affect your handling of all the other questions.

4) If the examination is of the essay type and contains but a few questions, it is a moot point as to whether you should read all the questions before starting to answer any one. Of course, if you are given a choice – say five out of seven and the like – then it is essential to read all the questions so you can eliminate the two that are most difficult. If, however, you are asked to answer all the questions, there may be danger in trying to answer the easiest one first because you may find that you will spend too much time on it. The best technique is to answer the first question, then proceed to the second, etc.

5) Time your answers. Before the exam begins, write down the time it started, then add the time allowed for the examination and write down the time it must be completed, then divide the time available somewhat as follows:
    - If 3-1/2 hours are allowed, that would be 210 minutes. If you have 80 objective-type questions, that would be an average of 2-1/2 minutes per question. Allow yourself no more than 2 minutes per question, or a total of 160 minutes, which will permit about 50 minutes to review.
    - If for the time allotment of 210 minutes there are 7 essay questions to answer, that would average about 30 minutes a question. Give yourself only 25 minutes per question so that you have about 35 minutes to review.

6) The most important instruction is to *read each question* and make sure you know what is wanted. The second most important instruction is to *time yourself properly* so that you answer every question. The third most important instruction is to *answer every question*. Guess if you have to but include something for each question. Remember that you will receive no credit for a blank and will probably receive some credit if you write something in answer to an essay question. If you guess a letter – say "B" for a multiple-choice question – you may have guessed right. If you leave a blank as an answer to a multiple-choice question, the examiners may respect your feelings but it will not add a point to your score. Some exams may penalize you for wrong answers, so in such cases *only*, you may not want to guess unless you have some basis for your answer.

7) Suggestions
    a. Objective-type questions
        1. Examine the question booklet for proper sequence of pages and questions
        2. Read all instructions carefully
        3. Skip any question which seems too difficult; return to it after all other questions have been answered
        4. Apportion your time properly; do not spend too much time on any single question or group of questions

5. Note and underline key words – *all, most, fewest, least, best, worst, same, opposite,* etc.
6. Pay particular attention to negatives
7. Note unusual option, e.g., unduly long, short, complex, different or similar in content to the body of the question
8. Observe the use of "hedging" words – *probably, may, most likely,* etc.
9. Make sure that your answer is put next to the same number as the question
10. Do not second-guess unless you have good reason to believe the second answer is definitely more correct
11. Cross out original answer if you decide another answer is more accurate; do not erase until you are ready to hand your paper in
12. Answer all questions; guess unless instructed otherwise
13. Leave time for review

   b. Essay questions
1. Read each question carefully
2. Determine exactly what is wanted. Underline key words or phrases.
3. Decide on outline or paragraph answer
4. Include many different points and elements unless asked to develop any one or two points or elements
5. Show impartiality by giving pros and cons unless directed to select one side only
6. Make and write down any assumptions you find necessary to answer the questions
7. Watch your English, grammar, punctuation and choice of words
8. Time your answers; don't crowd material

8) Answering the essay question

Most essay questions can be answered by framing the specific response around several key words or ideas. Here are a few such key words or ideas:

M's: manpower, materials, methods, money, management
P's: purpose, program, policy, plan, procedure, practice, problems, pitfalls, personnel, public relations

   a. Six basic steps in handling problems:
1. Preliminary plan and background development
2. Collect information, data and facts
3. Analyze and interpret information, data and facts
4. Analyze and develop solutions as well as make recommendations
5. Prepare report and sell recommendations
6. Install recommendations and follow up effectiveness

   b. Pitfalls to avoid
1. *Taking things for granted* – A statement of the situation does not necessarily imply that each of the elements is necessarily true; for example, a complaint may be invalid and biased so that all that can be taken for granted is that a complaint has been registered

2. *Considering only one side of a situation* – Wherever possible, indicate several alternatives and then point out the reasons you selected the best one
3. *Failing to indicate follow up* – Whenever your answer indicates action on your part, make certain that you will take proper follow-up action to see how successful your recommendations, procedures or actions turn out to be
4. *Taking too long in answering any single question* – Remember to time your answers properly

IX. AFTER THE TEST

Scoring procedures differ in detail among civil service jurisdictions although the general principles are the same. Whether the papers are hand-scored or graded by machine we have described, they are nearly always graded by number. That is, the person who marks the paper knows only the number – never the name – of the applicant. Not until all the papers have been graded will they be matched with names. If other tests, such as training and experience or oral interview ratings have been given, scores will be combined. Different parts of the examination usually have different weights. For example, the written test might count 60 percent of the final grade, and a rating of training and experience 40 percent. In many jurisdictions, veterans will have a certain number of points added to their grades.

After the final grade has been determined, the names are placed in grade order and an eligible list is established. There are various methods for resolving ties between those who get the same final grade – probably the most common is to place first the name of the person whose application was received first. Job offers are made from the eligible list in the order the names appear on it. You will be notified of your grade and your rank as soon as all these computations have been made. This will be done as rapidly as possible.

People who are found to meet the requirements in the announcement are called "eligibles." Their names are put on a list of eligible candidates. An eligible's chances of getting a job depend on how high he stands on this list and how fast agencies are filling jobs from the list.

When a job is to be filled from a list of eligibles, the agency asks for the names of people on the list of eligibles for that job. When the civil service commission receives this request, it sends to the agency the names of the three people highest on this list. Or, if the job to be filled has specialized requirements, the office sends the agency the names of the top three persons who meet these requirements from the general list.

The appointing officer makes a choice from among the three people whose names were sent to him. If the selected person accepts the appointment, the names of the others are put back on the list to be considered for future openings.

That is the rule in hiring from all kinds of eligible lists, whether they are for typist, carpenter, chemist, or something else. For every vacancy, the appointing officer has his choice of any one of the top three eligibles on the list. This explains why the person whose name is on top of the list sometimes does not get an appointment when some of the persons lower on the list do. If the appointing officer chooses the second or third eligible, the No. 1 eligible does not get a job at once, but stays on the list until he is appointed or the list is terminated.

X. HOW TO PASS THE INTERVIEW TEST

The examination for which you applied requires an oral interview test. You have already taken the written test and you are now being called for the interview test – the final part of the formal examination.

You may think that it is not possible to prepare for an interview test and that there are no procedures to follow during an interview. Our purpose is to point out some things you can do in advance that will help you and some good rules to follow and pitfalls to avoid while you are being interviewed.

What is an interview supposed to test?

The written examination is designed to test the technical knowledge and competence of the candidate; the oral is designed to evaluate intangible qualities, not readily measured otherwise, and to establish a list showing the relative fitness of each candidate – as measured against his competitors – for the position sought. Scoring is not on the basis of "right" and "wrong," but on a sliding scale of values ranging from "not passable" to "outstanding." As a matter of fact, it is possible to achieve a relatively low score without a single "incorrect" answer because of evident weakness in the qualities being measured.

Occasionally, an examination may consist entirely of an oral test – either an individual or a group oral. In such cases, information is sought concerning the technical knowledges and abilities of the candidate, since there has been no written examination for this purpose. More commonly, however, an oral test is used to supplement a written examination.

Who conducts interviews?

The composition of oral boards varies among different jurisdictions. In nearly all, a representative of the personnel department serves as chairman. One of the members of the board may be a representative of the department in which the candidate would work. In some cases, "outside experts" are used, and, frequently, a businessman or some other representative of the general public is asked to serve. Labor and management or other special groups may be represented. The aim is to secure the services of experts in the appropriate field.

However the board is composed, it is a good idea (and not at all improper or unethical) to ascertain in advance of the interview who the members are and what groups they represent. When you are introduced to them, you will have some idea of their backgrounds and interests, and at least you will not stutter and stammer over their names.

What should be done before the interview?

While knowledge about the board members is useful and takes some of the surprise element out of the interview, there is other preparation which is more substantive. It *is* possible to prepare for an oral interview – in several ways:

1) Keep a copy of your application and review it carefully before the interview

This may be the only document before the oral board, and the starting point of the interview. Know what education and experience you have listed there, and the sequence and dates of all of it. Sometimes the board will ask you to review the highlights of your experience for them; you should not have to hem and haw doing it.

2) Study the class specification and the examination announcement

Usually, the oral board has one or both of these to guide them. The qualities, characteristics or knowledges required by the position sought are stated in these documents. They offer valuable clues as to the nature of the oral interview. For example, if the job involves supervisory responsibilities, the announcement will usually indicate that knowledge of modern supervisory methods and the qualifications of the candidate as a supervisor will be tested. If so, you can expect such questions, frequently in the form of a hypothetical situation which you are expected to solve. NEVER go into an oral without knowledge of the duties and responsibilities of the job you seek.

3) Think through each qualification required

Try to visualize the kind of questions you would ask if you were a board member. How well could you answer them? Try especially to appraise your own knowledge and background in each area, *measured against the job sought*, and identify any areas in which you are weak. Be critical and realistic – do not flatter yourself.

4) Do some general reading in areas in which you feel you may be weak

For example, if the job involves supervision and your past experience has NOT, some general reading in supervisory methods and practices, particularly in the field of human relations, might be useful. Do NOT study agency procedures or detailed manuals. The oral board will be testing your understanding and capacity, not your memory.

5) Get a good night's sleep and watch your general health and mental attitude

You will want a clear head at the interview. Take care of a cold or any other minor ailment, and of course, no hangovers.

What should be done on the day of the interview?

Now comes the day of the interview itself. Give yourself plenty of time to get there. Plan to arrive somewhat ahead of the scheduled time, particularly if your appointment is in the fore part of the day. If a previous candidate fails to appear, the board might be ready for you a bit early. By early afternoon an oral board is almost invariably behind schedule if there are many candidates, and you may have to wait. Take along a book or magazine to read, or your application to review, but leave any extraneous material in the waiting room when you go in for your interview. In any event, relax and compose yourself.

The matter of dress is important. The board is forming impressions about you – from your experience, your manners, your attitude, and your appearance. Give your personal appearance careful attention. Dress your best, but not your flashiest. Choose conservative, appropriate clothing, and be sure it is immaculate. This is a business interview, and your appearance should indicate that you regard it as such. Besides, being well groomed and properly dressed will help boost your confidence.

Sooner or later, someone will call your name and escort you into the interview room. *This is it.* From here on you are on your own. It is too late for any more preparation. But remember, you asked for this opportunity to prove your fitness, and you are here because your request was granted.

What happens when you go in?

The usual sequence of events will be as follows: The clerk (who is often the board stenographer) will introduce you to the chairman of the oral board, who will introduce you to the other members of the board. Acknowledge the introductions before you sit down. Do not be surprised if you find a microphone facing you or a stenotypist sitting by. Oral interviews are usually recorded in the event of an appeal or other review.

Usually the chairman of the board will open the interview by reviewing the highlights of your education and work experience from your application – primarily for the benefit of the other members of the board, as well as to get the material into the record. Do not interrupt or comment unless there is an error or significant misinterpretation; if that is the case, do not hesitate. But do not quibble about insignificant matters. Also, he will usually ask you some question about your education, experience or your present job – partly to get you to start talking and to establish the interviewing "rapport." He may start the actual questioning, or turn it over to one of the other members. Frequently, each member undertakes the questioning on a particular area, one in which he is perhaps most competent, so you can expect each member to participate in the examination. Because time is limited, you may also expect some rather abrupt switches in the direction the questioning takes, so do not be upset by it. Normally, a board member will not pursue a single line of questioning unless he discovers a particular strength or weakness.

After each member has participated, the chairman will usually ask whether any member has any further questions, then will ask you if you have anything you wish to add. Unless you are expecting this question, it may floor you. Worse, it may start you off on an extended, extemporaneous speech. The board is not usually seeking more information. The question is principally to offer you a last opportunity to present further qualifications or to indicate that you have nothing to add. So, if you feel that a significant qualification or characteristic has been overlooked, it is proper to point it out in a sentence or so. Do not compliment the board on the thoroughness of their examination – they have been sketchy, and you know it. If you wish, merely say, "No thank you, I have nothing further to add." This is a point where you can "talk yourself out" of a good impression or fail to present an important bit of information. Remember, *you close the interview yourself*.

The chairman will then say, "That is all, Mr. _____, thank you." Do not be startled; the interview is over, and quicker than you think. Thank him, gather your belongings and take your leave. Save your sigh of relief for the other side of the door.

How to put your best foot forward

Throughout this entire process, you may feel that the board individually and collectively is trying to pierce your defenses, seek out your hidden weaknesses and embarrass and confuse you. Actually, this is not true. They are obliged to make an appraisal of your qualifications for the job you are seeking, and they want to see you in your best light. Remember, they must interview all candidates and a non-cooperative candidate may become a failure in spite of their best efforts to bring out his qualifications. Here are 15 suggestions that will help you:

1) Be natural – Keep your attitude confident, not cocky

If you are not confident that you can do the job, do not expect the board to be. Do not apologize for your weaknesses, try to bring out your strong points. The board is interested in a positive, not negative, presentation. Cockiness will antagonize any board member and make him wonder if you are covering up a weakness by a false show of strength.

2) Get comfortable, but don't lounge or sprawl

Sit erectly but not stiffly. A careless posture may lead the board to conclude that you are careless in other things, or at least that you are not impressed by the importance of the occasion. Either conclusion is natural, even if incorrect. Do not fuss with your clothing, a pencil or an ashtray. Your hands may occasionally be useful to emphasize a point; do not let them become a point of distraction.

3) Do not wisecrack or make small talk

This is a serious situation, and your attitude should show that you consider it as such. Further, the time of the board is limited – they do not want to waste it, and neither should you.

4) Do not exaggerate your experience or abilities

In the first place, from information in the application or other interviews and sources, the board may know more about you than you think. Secondly, you probably will not get away with it. An experienced board is rather adept at spotting such a situation, so do not take the chance.

5) If you know a board member, do not make a point of it, yet do not hide it

Certainly you are not fooling him, and probably not the other members of the board. Do not try to take advantage of your acquaintanceship – it will probably do you little good.

6) Do not dominate the interview

Let the board do that. They will give you the clues – do not assume that you have to do all the talking. Realize that the board has a number of questions to ask you, and do not try to take up all the interview time by showing off your extensive knowledge of the answer to the first one.

7) Be attentive

You only have 20 minutes or so, and you should keep your attention at its sharpest throughout. When a member is addressing a problem or question to you, give him your undivided attention. Address your reply principally to him, but do not exclude the other board members.

8) Do not interrupt

A board member may be stating a problem for you to analyze. He will ask you a question when the time comes. Let him state the problem, and wait for the question.

9) Make sure you understand the question

Do not try to answer until you are sure what the question is. If it is not clear, restate it in your own words or ask the board member to clarify it for you. However, do not haggle about minor elements.

10) Reply promptly but not hastily

A common entry on oral board rating sheets is "candidate responded readily," or "candidate hesitated in replies." Respond as promptly and quickly as you can, but do not jump to a hasty, ill-considered answer.

11) Do not be peremptory in your answers

A brief answer is proper – but do not fire your answer back. That is a losing game from your point of view. The board member can probably ask questions much faster than you can answer them.

12) Do not try to create the answer you think the board member wants

He is interested in what kind of mind you have and how it works – not in playing games. Furthermore, he can usually spot this practice and will actually grade you down on it.

13) Do not switch sides in your reply merely to agree with a board member

Frequently, a member will take a contrary position merely to draw you out and to see if you are willing and able to defend your point of view. Do not start a debate, yet do not surrender a good position. If a position is worth taking, it is worth defending.

14) Do not be afraid to admit an error in judgment if you are shown to be wrong

The board knows that you are forced to reply without any opportunity for careful consideration. Your answer may be demonstrably wrong. If so, admit it and get on with the interview.

15) Do not dwell at length on your present job

The opening question may relate to your present assignment. Answer the question but do not go into an extended discussion. You are being examined for a *new* job, not your present one. As a matter of fact, try to phrase ALL your answers in terms of the job for which you are being examined.

Basis of Rating

Probably you will forget most of these "do's" and "don'ts" when you walk into the oral interview room. Even remembering them all will not ensure you a passing grade. Perhaps you did not have the qualifications in the first place. But remembering them will help you to put your best foot forward, without treading on the toes of the board members.

Rumor and popular opinion to the contrary notwithstanding, an oral board wants you to make the best appearance possible. They know you are under pressure – but they also want to see how you respond to it as a guide to what your reaction would be under the pressures of the job you seek. They will be influenced by the degree of poise you display, the personal traits you show and the manner in which you respond.

ABOUT THIS BOOK

This book contains tests divided into Examination Sections. Go through each test, answering every question in the margin. We have also attached a sample answer sheet at the back of the book that can be removed and used. At the end of each test look at the answer key and check your answers. On the ones you got wrong, look at the right answer choice and learn. Do not fill in the answers first. Do not memorize the questions and answers, but understand the answer and principles involved. On your test, the questions will likely be different from the samples. Questions are changed and new ones added. If you understand these past questions you should have success with any changes that arise. Tests may consist of several types of questions. We have additional books on each subject should more study be advisable or necessary for you. Finally, the more you study, the better prepared you will be. This book is intended to be the last thing you study before you walk into the examination room. Prior study of relevant texts is also recommended. NLC publishes some of these in our Fundamental Series. Knowledge and good sense are important factors in passing your exam. Good luck also helps. So now study this Passbook, absorb the material contained within and take that knowledge into the examination. Then do your best to pass that exam.

EXAMINATION SECTION

EXAMINATION SECTION

TEST 1

DIRECTIONS: Each question or incomplete statement is followed by several suggested answers or completions. Select the one that BEST answers the question or completes the statement. *PRINT THE LETTER OF THE CORRECT ANSWER IN THE SPACE AT THE RIGHT.*

1. You are assisting with the care of a patient who is suffering from false sensory perceptions and is completely out of touch with reality. These perceptions are referred to as
    A. visions
    B. delusions
    C. hallucinations
    D. flashbacks

    1._____

2. A suicidal patient needs assistance to the bathroom. How should you act when dealing with this situation?
    A. Closely observe the patient
    B. Allow the patient privacy while in the bathroom
    C. Permit the patient to shave
    D. Make sure all sharp items have been removed from the room

    2._____

3. Which of the following is important when caring for a patient with anorexia nervosa?
    A. Allow the patient to have privacy during meal times
    B. Patients should adhere to a strict meal plan
    C. No visitors should be permitted until the patient begins to eat normally
    D. You should be present at all times to make sure the patient eats

    3._____

4. A recently widowed woman is dealing with severe depression and is possibly suicidal. Which of the following questions would be appropriate in order to determine whether or not the patient is suicidal?
    A. "Why do you want to kill yourself?"
    B. "How would you kill yourself?"
    C. "Are you sure you want to kill yourself?"
    D. "Where would you kill yourself?"

    4._____

5. Which of the following characteristics would be evident for a patient who is abusing opiates such as morphine?
    A. Euphoria and dilated pupils
    B. High energy and dilated pupils
    C. Anger and constricted pupils
    D. Slurred speech and dilated pupils

    5._____

6. What is the appropriate action when a patient is having an anxiety attack?
    A. Stay with the patient and speak calmly and slowly
    B. Open windows and turn on lights to avoid claustrophobia
    C. Leave the patient alone in silence
    D. Turn on soothing music

    6._____

7. If a patient has delusions of grandeur, what does this refer to?
   A. The patient feels that he/she is extremely important
   B. The patient is experiencing hallucinations
   C. The patient is suicidal
   D. The patient is severely depressed

8. Enforcing limits on behavior is most important for what type of patient?
   A. Depressed
   B. Suicidal
   C. Anxious
   D. Manic

9. What are signs and symptoms of post-traumatic stress disorder?
   A. Hostility and violence
   B. Behavior changes and anorexia
   C. Hyper alertness and insomnia
   D. Memory loss and insomnia

10. Which of the following is appropriate for a patient with manic depression?
    A. Encouraging the patient to eat high calorie meals
    B. Insisting on highly exertional activities so patient sleeps at night
    C. Listening closely and avoiding power struggles
    D. Allowing patient to behave with no limits

11. A patient with post-traumatic stress disorder is experiencing nightmares, depression, alcohol abuse, and feelings of hopelessness. Which of the following is important for relieving the symptoms of this patient?
    A. Regular attendance at Alcoholics Anonymous meetings
    B. Family support
    C. Proper anti-anxiety medicine
    D. Encouraging patient to talk about the past experiences

12. If a patient is undergoing detoxification for a heroin overdose and states they can stop using heroin if they want to is an example of which coping mechanism?
    A. Repression
    B. Delusion
    C. Denial
    D. Withdrawal

13. What is a common characteristic among patients who suffer from dependent personality disorder?
    A. Cannot form lasting relationships
    B. Cannot make decisions without seeking advice
    C. Self-destructive behavior
    D. Hopelessness

14. Which of the following is an early sign of alcohol withdrawal?
    A. Slurred speech
    B. Perceptual disorders
    C. Agitation
    D. Depression

15. Which of the following is a characteristic of a patient with schizotypal personality disorder when faced with a social situation?
    A. Paranoia
    B. Depression
    C. Agitation
    D. Homicidal impulses

16. When a patient is in a manic state, what is the MOST appropriate action to relieve this situation?
    A. Encourage patient to express feelings
    B. Discourage interaction with other people until manic state passes
    C. Encourage interaction with others to relieve manic state
    D. Reduce any stimulation that may contribute to the manic state

17. Which of the following is imperative in order to care for a patient with bulimia?
    A. Determine which situations cause anxiety
    B. Determine why the patient feels they need to lose weight
    C. Determine what foods the patient likes to eat
    D. Restrict patients to three planned meals per day

18. Which of the following behaviors is indicative of adult cognitive development?
    A. Generating new levels of awareness
    B. Assuming responsibility for actions
    C. Can solve problems and learn new skills
    D. Has reality-based perceptions

19. Which of the following is common when a patient first begins to take lithium for treatment of bipolar disorder?
    A. Excessive thirst
    B. Excessive urination
    C. Constipation
    D. Excessive hunger

20. What characteristics are common for a patient who has overdosed on amphetamines?
    A. Low pulse rate
    B. Low blood pressure
    C. Slurred speech
    D. Irritability

21. Which medications are appropriate for treating patients who commonly suffer from panic attacks?
    A. Opiates
    B. Anti-depressants
    C. Anti-anxiety medications
    D. Barbiturates

22. What is the BEST course of action when a patient is actively having hallucinations that are causing agitation?
    A. Try to bring the patient back to reality
    B. Give the patient a sedative
    C. Try to find out the content of the hallucination
    D. Immediately restrain the patient

23. What is the BEST course of action when a patient with paranoid schizophrenia gets upset and tells you to leave him alone?
    A. Explain that you are in control, not the patient
    B. Continue to do your job regardless of the patient's feelings
    C. Explain that you will leave for now but be back soon
    D. Find out why the patient wants to be left alone

24. What condition is characterized by tonic contractures of the muscles of the neck, mouth, and tongue?
    A. Dystonia
    B. Dyskinesia
    C. Heroin overdose
    D. Cocaine overdose

25. Which blood electrolyte level is important to monitor before a patient begins to take lithium?
    A. Potassium   B. Sodium   C. Calcium   D. Chloride

KEY (CORRECT ANSWERS)

1.	C	11.	D
2.	A	12.	C
3.	B	13.	B
4.	B	14.	B
5.	D	15.	A
6.	A	16.	D
7.	A	17.	A
8.	D	18.	A
9.	C	19.	B
10.	C	20.	D

21. C
22. C
23. C
24. A
25. B

TEST 2

DIRECTIONS: Each question or incomplete statement is followed by several suggested answers or completions. Select the one that BEST answers the question or completes the statement. *PRINT THE LETTER OF THE CORRECT ANSWER IN THE SPACE AT THE RIGHT.*

1. Which of the following is defined as the state of well-being where a person can realize his own abilities and cope with normal stresses of life and work?
    A. Mental illness
    B. Mental health
    C. Physical health
    D. Emotional health

2. Which duty is appropriately performed by a mental health technician?
    A. Administering medications to a patient
    B. Coordinating the overall care for a patient
    C. Providing information regarding alcohol abuse
    D. Prescribing medications for treatment of a patient

3. If a patient states, "Give me a few minutes to remember," this patient is operating on which of the following?
    A. Conscious
    B. Subconscious
    C. Unconscious
    D. Ego

4. Which of the following is a characteristic of the superego portion of the psyche?
    A. It is the censoring portion of the mind
    B. It is impulsive and lacks morals
    C. It analyzes prior to making decisions
    D. It uses defensive functions for protection

5. Which of the following characteristics is associated with the primary level of prevention?
    A. Rehabilitating a patient to take care of himself
    B. Making sure a suicidal patient cannot harm himself
    C. Performing community-wide disease surveillance
    D. Teaching a patient how to deal with stress

6. If you suspect a woman and a child are victims of abuse, which of the following questions is MOST appropriate for you to ask?
    A. "Are you okay?"
    B. "Is something bothering you?"
    C. "What happened to you?"
    D. "Are you being threatened or hurt by your partner?"

7. Sexual _____ disorder would be characterized by a female abuse victim who develops a diminished sex drive.
    A. pain
    B. arousal
    C. desire
    D. appetite

8. If a patient is still living with an abusive spouse, what is the BEST advice you can offer?
   A. Tell the patient to end the relationship
   B. Tell the patient to summon the family's opinion regarding the relationship
   C. Give the patient information for a crisis center
   D. Tell the patient what you would do if you were in the same situation

9. Which of the following statements could indicate child abuse if made by a parent?
   A. "If I tell my child to do something once, I better not have to tell them again."
   B. "My child tells me no all the time."
   C. "Once my child is potty trained, I can still expect an accident from time to time."
   D. "I encourage my children to try new and different things."

10. What is the PRIMARY concern when dealing with a victim of child abuse?
    A. Understand why the child is being abused
    B. Make sure the patient is safe from further harm
    C. Make sure the patient is now comfortable
    D. Teach the victim how to mentally deal with the abuse

11. Which somatoform disorder is characterized by constant complaints of pain or illness without any medical or clinical explanation?
    A. Hypochondriasis   B. Conversion disorder
    C. Somatization disorder   D. Somatoform Pain disorder

12. According to Sigmund Freud, anxiety is defined as
    A. conflict between the id and superego
    B. a hypothalamic-pituitary-adrenal reaction to stress
    C. a conditioned response to stress
    D. functions to satisfy the need for security

13. Which of the following medications would be appropriate for reducing the symptoms of alcohol withdrawal?
    A. Narcan   B. Librium   C. Haldol   D. Phenobarbital

14. Parents of children who develop anorexia nervosa commonly have which of the following characteristics?
    A. History of drug abuse
    B. Generally ignoring their children
    C. Tendency to be strict and overprotective
    D. Tendency to be extremely aggressive and goal oriented

15. What is the FIRST priority when dealing with a spousal abuse victim and the spouse shows up to *finish the job*?
    A. Confront the abusing spouse
    B. Remain with the victim and stay calm
    C. Call security and another staff member for assistance
    D. Ask the abusing spouse why this happened

16. Which aspect is very important when dealing with a patient with bulimia in which strict management of dietary intake is necessary?
    A. Allowing the patient to eat meals in private
    B. Allowing the patient to choose their own food and staying with them for an hour after the meal is finished
    C. Choosing the food for the patient and making sure they eat at least half of the meal
    D. Keeping patient engaged in activities for two hours after each meal time

17. Patients being treated with Antabuse need to carefully read the labels on which products to avoid potential reactions?
    A. Sodas
    B. Cologne and aftershaves
    C. Toothpaste
    D. Juices

18. If you are caring for an injured child, what specific action would lead you to believe the child is being abused?
    The child
    A. does not cry when being examined
    B. does not make eye contact with the caregiver
    C. cries uncontrollably throughout the examination
    D. resists contact from the caregiver

19. The patient's _____ needs is the highest priority when encountering a patient who has taken PCP.
    A. medical
    B. psychological
    C. physical
    D. safety

20. How would you proceed if you entered a room and found a patient sitting on the floor with cuts on both wrists and surrounded by broken glass?
    A. Approach the patient slowly, speak in a calm voice, call the patient by name and tell them you are here to help
    B. Move the glass away and sit down next to the patient
    C. Call for additional staff before entering the room and restraining the patient
    D. Enter the room quietly and get beside the patient to assess him

21. Clonidine is useful for treating which condition other than hypertension?
    A. Alcohol withdrawal
    B. Opiate withdrawal
    C. Cocaine withdrawal
    D. Heroin withdrawal

22. Which of the following are early signs of alcohol withdrawal? 22.____
    A. Sweating, tremors, nervousness
    B. Hypertension, sweating, seizures
    C. Dehydration, fever, itching
    D. Vomiting, diarrhea, slow heart rate

23. What are some behavioral characteristics for a person with antisocial personality disorder? 23.____
    A. Continuously talks of violence
    B. Silence and disobedient
    C. Rigid posture, restlessness, glaring
    D. Depression and physical withdrawal

24. How long after the last alcoholic drink will early withdrawal symptoms begin to become evident? 24.____
    A. 6 hours			B. 12 hours
    C. 24-48 hours		D. 60-72 hours

25. What is the proper treatment for a patient experiencing hallucinations secondary to alcohol abuse? 25.____
    A. Keep patient restrained until hallucinations stop
    B. Check blood pressure every 15 minutes and force fluids
    C. Keep environment calm and quiet and give medications as needed
    D. Continuously monitor the patient and check blood pressure every 30 minutes

KEY (CORRECT ANSWERS)

1.	B		11.	D
2.	A		12.	A
3.	B		13.	B
4.	A		14.	C
5.	D		15.	C
6.	D		16.	B
7.	C		17.	B
8.	C		18.	A
9.	A		19.	D
10.	B		20.	A

21. B
22. D
23. C
24. C
25. C

EXAMINATION SECTION
TEST 1

DIRECTIONS: Each question or incomplete statement is followed by several suggested answers or completions. Select the one that BEST answers the question or completes the statement. *PRINT THE LETTER OF THE CORRECT ANSWER IN THE SPACE AT THE RIGHT.*

1. Which of the following findings is MOST consistent with early alcohol withdrawal?
    A. Heart rate of 50-60 beats per minute
    B. Heart rate of 120-140 beats per minute
    C. Blood pressure of 90/60 mmHg
    D. Blood pressure of 140/80 mmHg

1.____

2. Which of the following patients would have the HIGHEST risk for suicide?
    A. Patient who talks about wanting to die
    B. Patient who plans a violent death and has the means to do so
    C. Patient who appears depressed, frequently thinks about dying, and gives away all personal possessions
    D. Patient who says they may do something if life does not improve soon

2.____

3. Which medical condition is commonly associated with patients with bulimia nervosa?
    A. Diabetes   B. HIV   C. Cancer   D. Hepatitis C

3.____

4. What action would be considered as a primary nursing intervention for a victim of child abuse?
    A. Teach the victim coping skills
    B. Ensure the safety of the victim
    C. Analyze the family dynamics
    D. Assess the scope of the problem

4.____

5. Somatoform disorder is defined as
    A. management consisting of a specific medical treatment
    B. expression of conflicts through bodily symptoms
    C. a voluntary expression of psychological conflicts
    D. physical symptoms explained by organic causes

5.____

6. What is a proper plan for treating a school-age child with attention deficit hyperactivity disorder?
    A. Ignore the child's hyperactivity
    B. Child should be removed from the classroom when disruptive
    C. Child should have as much structure as possible
    D. Encourage the child to play to release excess energy

6.____

7. Which characteristic is common for a child with conduct disorder? 7.____
   A. Ritualistic behaviors
   B. Preference for inanimate objects
   C. Severe violations of age-related normal behavior
   D. Easily distracted

8. School phobia is commonly relieved by 8.____
   A. allowing the parent to be with the child in the classroom
   B. immediately returning the child to school with a family member
   C. telling the student why attendance at school is important
   D. allowing the child to enter the school before the other children

9. If a child has an I.Q. of 45, what classification of mental retardation does this value represent? 9.____
   A. Mild   B. Moderate   C. Severe   D. Profound

10. Which characteristics are common for a child with autistic disorder? 10.____
    A. Aggression, stealing, lying
    B. Easily distracted, impulsive, and hyperactive
    C. Intolerant to change, disturbed relatedness, stereotypes
    D. Angry, argumentative, and disobedient

11. Which of the following would NOT be an acceptable therapeutic approach for caring for an autistic child? 11.____
    A. Providing safety measures
    B. Rearranging the environment to motivate the child
    C. Engaging a diversion when acting out
    D. Providing an atmosphere of acceptance

12. According to Piaget's Cognitive Stages of Development, a 5-year-old child is in what stage of development? 12.____
    A. Sensorimotor stage   B. Concrete operations
    C. Pre-operational   D. Formal operation

13. What is indicated if a patient states they have to increase their level of alcohol intake to achieve the desired effect? 13.____
    A. Tolerance   B. Withdrawal
    C. Intoxication   D. Weight gain

14. If an alcoholic patient is experiencing tremors, irritability, hypertension, and fever, what condition will soon follow? 14.____
    A. Esophageal varices   B. Korsakoff's syndrome
    C. Wernicke's syndrome   D. Delirium tremens

15. What would be the proper treatment for a patient in delirium tremens? 15.____
    A. Adequate fluids and high nutrient foods
    B. Placed in a quiet, dimly lit room
    C. Administration of Librium
    D. Monitoring vital signs every hour

16. If a patient presents with hallucinations, agitation, and an irritated nasal septum, which illicit drug did the patient MOST likely ingest?
    A. Marijuana
    B. Cocaine
    C. Heroin
    D. Methamphetamine

16.____

17. What would be the appropriate medication for a patient who presents with needle tracks in the arm, in a stupor, and with a pinpoint pupil?
    A. Narcan   B. Methadone   C. Naltrexone   D. Disulfiram

17.____

18. If an elderly patient presents with increasing forgetfulness, decreasing daily function, and using a toothbrush to comb his hair, which of the following conditions is being exhibited by this patient?
    A. Aphasia   B. Amnesia   C. Apraxia   D. Agnosia

18.____

19. What would be a PRIMARY treatment intervention for a patient with moderate stage dementia?
    A. Providing a safe and secure environment
    B. Providing adequate nutrition and hydration
    C. Encouraging memories to decrease isolation
    D. Encouraging to independently care for themselves

19.____

20. Through which characteristic is dementia different from delirium?
    A. Dementia promotes slurred speech
    B. Dementia has a gradual onset
    C. Dementia includes clouding of the consciousness
    D. Dementia includes a sensory perceptual change

20.____

21. What would be the BEST advice you could give to a patient who feels the need to starve themselves?
    A. Exercise until the need to starve passes
    B. Allow the patient to starve to relieve anxiety
    C. Tell the patient's family immediately
    D. Tell the patient to approach a nurse and talk out their feelings

21.____

22. Which characteristic is a sign of improvement for patients with anorexia nervosa?
    A. Weight loss
    B. Weight gain
    C. Eating meals in the dining room
    D. Participation in group activities

22.____

23. What is the MAJOR difference between anorexia nervosa and bulimia nervosa?
    Bulimic patients
    A. will have periods of binge eating and purging
    B. will have lesser anxiety
    C. will have peculiar food handling patterns
    D. have poor self-esteem

23.____

24. A caregiver can build a therapeutic relationship with a bulimic patient by performing all of the following actions EXCEPT
    A. discussing their eating behavior
    B. establishing an atmosphere of trust
    C. helping patients identify feelings associated with binging and purging
    D. educating the patient about the condition of bulimia nervosa

25. Which condition would be characterized by an intense fear of riding in an elevator?
    A. Arachnophobia
    B. Agoraphobia
    C. Xenophobia
    D. Claustrophobia

KEY (CORRECT ANSWERS)

1.	B		11.	B
2.	B		12.	C
3.	A		13.	A
4.	C		14.	D
5.	B		15.	D
6.	C		16.	B
7.	C		17.	A
8.	B		18.	D
9.	B		19.	A
10.	C		20.	B

21. D
22. B
23. A
24. A
25. D

TEST 2

DIRECTIONS: Each question or incomplete statement is followed by several suggested answers or completions. Select the one that BEST answers the question or completes the statement. *PRINT THE LETTER OF THE CORRECT ANSWER IN THE SPACE AT THE RIGHT.*

1. What should be the INITIAL treatment action for a patient with claustrophobia?
   A. Accept the patient's fear without opinion or criticism
   B. Assist the patient to find the cause of the fear
   C. Allow the patient to talk about their fear as much as possible
   D. Establish a trusting relationship

   1._____

2. Which is evidence of a caregiver developing a countertransference reaction?
   A. Confronting the patient about discrepancies in their behavior
   B. Revealing personal information to the patient
   C. Focusing on the feelings of the patient
   D. Ignoring the patient's wants and needs

   2._____

3. In attempting to be accomplished when conducting desensitization, the patient
   A. stops using illicit drugs
   B. stops abusing alcohol
   C. overcomes disabling fear
   D. admits to all wrongdoings

   3._____

4. Which of the following should you advise patients who are prescribed to take valium?
   A. Increase fluid intake
   B. Decrease fluid intake
   C. Avoid caffeinated beverages
   D. Avoid alcoholic beverages

   4._____

5. How does malingering differ from somatoform disorder?
   A. Malingering is stress that is expressed through physical symptoms
   B. Malingering is gratification from the environment
   C. Malingering has evidence from an organic basis
   D. Malingering is a deliberate effort to handle upsetting events

   5._____

6. What is the MOST successful form of therapy for a somatoform disorder?
   A. Prescription medications
   B. Stress management
   C. Psychotherapy
   D. Milieu therapy

   6._____

7. What method would you use to treat a psychiatric patient who speaks a foreign language?
   A. Use pictures to communicate
   B. Speak in universal phrases
   C. Simply use nonverbal communication
   D. Employ the services of an interpreter

   7._____

8. The _____ theory attempts to explain obsessive compulsive behaviors related to unconscious conflicts between id impulses and the superego.
   A. cognitive
   B. psychoanalytic
   C. behavioral
   D. interpersonal

9. _____ the patient's obsessive compulsive disorder is the MOST successful behavior when caring for a patient with obsessive-compulsive disorder?
   A. Rejecting   B. Preventing   C. Accepting   D. Challenging

10. Which of the following characteristics would NOT be a factor for a patient having diminished sexual arousal?
    A. Medications
    B. Health status
    C. Education and work history
    D. Relationship with spouse

11. Getting the patient to _____ is the ultimate goal of treating a patient with somatoform disorder.
    A. take the prescribed medications
    B. recognize the signs and symptoms of physical illness
    C. cope with physical illness
    D. express anxiety verbally rather than through physical symptoms

12. What is MOST important when counseling a family whose teenage son has just been diagnosed with schizophrenia?
    A. The distressing symptoms of schizophrenia can respond to medications.
    B. Symptoms of this disease imbalance the brain.
    C. Genetic history is a factor for developing schizophrenia.
    D. Schizophrenia can affect every aspect of a patient's functioning.

13. A patient who states they only abuse alcohol and cocaine to deal with a stressful marriage and stressful job is exhibiting which defense mechanism?
    A. Displacement
    B. Rationalization
    C. Sublimation
    D. Projection

14. A pregnant female continues to use heroin throughout her pregnancy. Which of the following conditions would this child be at risk for developing?
    A. Heroin dependence
    B. Mental retardation
    C. Schizophrenia
    D. Anorexia nervosa

15. What is the MOST important medical intervention when caring for a victim of sexual assault?
    A. Preserving an unbroken chain of evidence
    B. Preserving the patient's privacy
    C. Determining the identity of the attacker
    D. Assessing for sexually transmitted diseases

16. Which of the following is NOT a factor for a victim of family violence to safely remain in the home?
    A. Ability of patient to relocate
    B. Socioeconomic status of the family
    C. Availability of community shelters
    D. A non-abusive family member to intervene on behalf of the victim

17. Inability to _____ would be a sign of early onset of Alzheimer's disease.
    A. balance a checkbook
    B. take care of self
    C. relate to family members
    D. remember own name

18. Which neurotransmitter is responsible for the development of Alzheimer's disease?
    A. Serotonin
    B. Dopamine
    C. Epinephrine
    D. Acetylcholine

19. What products should be avoided by patients who are taking lithium carbonate to stabilize moods?
    A. Caffeine   B. Diuretics   C. Antacids   D. Antibiotics

20. Which of the following situations would NOT increase stress on a healthy family system?
    A. Birth of a child
    B. Parental arguments
    C. Child going away to college
    D. Death of a grandparent

21. Patients who take monoamine oxidase inhibitors as antidepressants should avoid
    A. dairy and green vegetables
    B. red meat and poultry
    C. aged cheese and red wine
    D. flour, grains, and rice

22. What should a caregiver assess prior to administering thorazine to an agitated patient?
    A. Pulse rate
    B. Blood pressure
    C. Blood urea nitrogen level
    D. Liver enzymes

23. A patient who is prescribed benzodiazepine oxazepam should avoid excessive consumption of
    A. shellfish   B. coffee   C. sugar   D. salt

24. What is the PRIMARY purpose of Alcoholics Anonymous?
    A. Teach positive coping mechanisms
    B. Alleviate stress
    C. Help members maintain sobriety
    D. Provide fellowship among members

25. What would be the initial treatment intervention if a patient experiences   25.____
    a panic attack in your presence?
    A. Remain with patient and promote a safe environment
    B. Reduce external stimuli
    C. Encourage physical activity
    D. Teach coping mechanisms

KEY (CORRECT ANSWERS)

1. A
2. B
3. C
4. D
5. D

6. B
7. D
8. B
9. C
10. C

11. D
12. A
13. B
14. A
15. A

16. B
17. A
18. D
19. B
20. B

21. C
22. B
23. B
24. C
25. A

EXAMINATION SECTION
TEST 1

DIRECTIONS: Each question or incomplete statement is followed by several suggested answers or completions. Select the one that BEST answers the question or completes the statement. *PRINT THE LETTER OF THE CORRECT ANSWER IN THE SPACE AT THE RIGHT.*

1. The causes of abnormal behavior include

    A. alcohol and drugs
    B. head injuries and severe infection
    C. diabetes and psychiatric problems
    D. all of the above

2. All of the following are common reactions to anxiety EXCEPT

    A. depression
    B. flight of ideas
    C. denial
    D. regression

3. Of the following infections, the one which does NOT produce psychotic syndrome is

    A. chancroid
    B. brain abscess
    C. syphilis
    D. toxoplasmosis

4. In dealing with emotionally disturbed patients, an EMT should

    A. not assess the patient's needs
    B. intervene in the situation to the extent to which he feels capable
    C. overreact to the patient's behavior or emotional attacks
    D. none of the above

5. Crisis situations, including periods of _____, may affect the paramedic adversely.

    A. anxiety
    B. anger
    C. impatience
    D. all of the above

6. A professional attitude MUST be maintained while the paramedic is dealing with emotionally disturbed patients. This attitude can be characterized by all of the following EXCEPT

    A. anger
    B. warmth
    C. sensitivity
    D. compassion

7. The common emotional difficulties of the paramedic may be managed by

    A. discussing problems and anxieties with co-workers
    B. developing a regular discussion rap session with peers to discuss good and bad experiences
    C. discussing problems with the supervisor
    D. all of the above

8. There are certain general guidelines for dealing with any patient with a psychiatric problem.
   The one of the following which is NOT among these guidelines is:

   A. Be prepared to spend time with the disturbed patient.
   B. Be as calm and direct as possibl
   C. You do not need to identify yoursel
   D. Assess the patient wherever the emergency occurs.

9. Disorders of motor activity include all of the following EXCEPT

   A. agitation   B. compulsion
   C. perservation   D. restlessness

10. A repetitive action carried out to relieve the anxiety of obsessive thought is called

    A. compulsion   B. delirium
    C. confrontation   D. confabulation

11. The invention of experiences to cover over gaps in memory, seen in patients with certain organic brain syndromes, is

    A. dementia   B. confabulation
    C. psychosis   D. delusion

12. Among the following, which is NOT a symptom of a panic attack?

    A. Shortness of breath or a sensation of being smothered
    B. Feeling of unreality or of stepping apart from oneself
    C. Constant fatigue and no motivation to do anything
    D. Fear of dying and of being crazy

13. Risk factors for violence do NOT include

    A. any place where alcohol is being consumed
    B. natural death in the family
    C. crowd incidents
    D. incidents where violence has already occurred (e.g., shooting, stabbing)

14. Disorders of thinking include all of the following EXCEPT

    A. flight of ideas   B. retardation of thought
    C. compulsions   D. perseveration

15. All of the following are disorders of consciousness EXCEPT

    A. amnesia   B. delirium
    C. fugue stage   D. stupor and coma

16. A repetition of movements that don,t seem to serve any useful purpose is called

    A. compulsion   B. echolalia
    C. stereotyped activity D. all of the above

17. The definition of *compulsion* is:

    A. A repetitive action carried out to relieve the anxiety of obsessive thought
    B. The situation in which a patient cannot sit still
    C. Condition in which the patient echoes the words of the examiner
    D. None of the above

18. The MOST profound disorder of memory is

    A. confabulation
    B. amnesia
    C. illusion
    D. hallucination

19. An acute state of confusion characterized by global impairment of thinking, perception, and memory is called

    A. delusion   B. delirium   C. psychosis   D. dementia

20. Proper pre-hospital management of the manic patient includes

    A. not arguing or getting into a power struggle with the patient
    B. talking to a patient in a quiet place, away from other people
    C. consulting medical command if the patient refuses transport
    D. all of the above

Questions 21-25.

DIRECTIONS: In Questions 21 through 25, match the numbered definition with the lettered disorder, listed in Column I, that it MOST accurately describes. Place the letter of the CORRECT answer in the appropriate space at the right.

COLUMN I
A. Echolalia
B. Illusion
C. Delusion
D. Hallucination
E. Mood

21. Misinterpretation of sensory stimuli

22. False belief

23. Meaningless echoing of the interviewer's words by the patient

24. Sustained and pervasive emotional state

25. Sense of perception not founded on objective reality

KEY (CORRECT ANSWERS)

1. D
2. B
3. A
4. B
5. D

6. A
7. D
8. C
9. C
10. A

11. B
12. C
13. B
14. C
15. A

16. C
17. A
18. B
19. B
20. D

21. B
22. C
23. A
24. E
25. D

TEST 2

DIRECTIONS: Each question or incomplete statement is followed by several suggested answers or completions. Select the one that BEST answers the question or completes the statement. *PRINT THE LETTER OF THE CORRECT ANSWER IN THE SPACE AT THE RIGHT.*

1. The depressed patient can often be readily identified by

    A. a sad expression
    B. bouts of crying
    C. expression of feelings of worthlessness
    D. all of the above

2. The third leading cause of death among the 15- to 25 year-old age group is

    A. diabetes mellitus   B. rheumatoid arthritis
    C. suicide   D. congenital heart disease

3. The assessment of every depressed person MUST include an evaluation of

    A. schizophrenia
    B. suicide risk
    C. chronic debilitating illness
    D. anxiety

4. When caring for a patient who is displaying typical stress reactions, you should

    A. act in a calm manner, giving the patient time to gain control of his emotions
    B. quietly and carefully evaluate the situation
    C. stay alert for sudden changes in behavior
    D. all of the above

5. The patient in a psychiatric emergency is far more out of reach and out of control than the person in an emotional emergency.
   In a psychiatric emergency, the patient may do all of the following EXCEPT

    A. try to hurt himself
    B. try to seek help for protection
    C. withdraw, no longer responding to people or to his environment
    D. continue to act depressed, sometimes crying and expressing feelings of worthlessness

6. When a patient is acting as if he may hurt himself or another, you should do all of the following EXCEPT

    A. alert the police
    B. not isolate yourself from your partner or other sources of help
    C. try to restrain the patient by yourself
    D. always be on the watch for weapons

7. A mental disorder characterized by loss of contact with reality is called

    A. psychosis   B. dementia
    C. phobia   D. none of the above

8. Anti-psychotic drugs are also called

   A. antidepressants
   B. neuroleptics
   C. anxiolytics
   D. antiepileptics

9. The patient who hears voices commanding him to hurt himself or others must be considered

   A. normal
   B. safe
   C. dangerous
   D. none of the above

10. When in a state of *conversion hysteria,* a person's

    A. reaction may move from extreme anxiety to relative calmness
    B. may transform anxiety to some bodily function
    C. often becomes hysterically blind, deaf, or paralyzed
    D. all of the above

11. Repeating the same idea over and over again is called

    A. perseveration
    B. compulsion
    C. obsession
    D. facilitation

12. _____ is the interviewing technique in which the interviewer encourages the patient to proceed by noncommittal words and gestures.

    A. Echolalia
    B. Facilitation
    C. Affect
    D. None of the above

13. The CHRONIC deterioration of mental function is referred to as

    A. dementia
    B. psychosis
    C. delirium
    D. schizophrenia

14. A persistent idea that a person CANNOT dismiss from his thought is a(n)

    A. affect
    B. obsession
    C. compulsion
    D. delusion

15. An interviewing technique in which the interviewer points out to the patient something of interest in his conversation or behavior is

    A. facilitation
    B. confabulation
    C. confrontation
    D. perseveration

16. It is important for paramedics to be aware of one particular syndrome that may occur in patients taking anti-psychotic medication. This condition is

    A. acute diuresis
    B. acute dystonic reaction
    C. hypertensive crises
    D. none of the above

17. An acute dystonic reaction can be rapidly corrected by

    A. chlorpromazine
    B. prolixin
    C. diphenhydramine
    D. tindal

18. Tranquilizers are also called 18._____

    A. neuroleptics   B. anxiolytics
    C. chinergics   D. stimulants

19. The COMMON symptoms of antipsychotic drugs include 19._____

    A. blurred vision   B. dry mouth
    C. cardiac dysrhythmias   D. all of the above

20. Uncontrolled, disconnected thoughts characterize a dis organized patient who may be 20._____

    A. incoherent or rambling in his speech
    B. wandering aimlessly
    C. dressed inappropriately
    D. all of the above

Questions 21-25.

DIRECTIONS: In Questions 21 through 25, match the numbered definition with the lettered disorder, listed in Column I, that it MOST accurately describes. Place the letter of the CORRECT answer in the appropriate space at the right.

COLUMN I
A. Agitation
B. Agoraphobia
C. Flight of ideas
D. Neologism
E. Confabulation

21. Fear of the marketplace 21._____

22. An invented word that has meaning only to its inventor 22._____

23. The invention of experiences to cover over gaps in memory 23._____

24. Extreme restlessness and anxiety 24._____

25. Accelerated thinking in which the mind skips very rapidly from one thought to the next 25._____

KEY (CORRECT ANSWERS)

1. D
2. C
3. B
4. D
5. B

6. C
7. A
8. B
9. C
10. D

11. A
12. B
13. A
14. B
15. C

16. B
17. C
18. B
19. D
20. D

21. B
22. D
23. E
24. A
25. C

EXAMINATION SECTION
TEST 1

DIRECTIONS: Each question or incomplete statement is followed by several suggested answers or completions. Select the one that BEST answers the question or completes the statement. *PRINT THE LETTER OF THE CORRECT ANSWER IN THE SPACE AT THE RIGHT.*

1. A relationship in which a patient becomes dependent on the nurse   1.____

    A. is always unprofessional
    B. is inevitably "bad" for the patient
    C. may be necessary temporarily
    D. impedes learning

2. Anxiety is the CHIEF characteristic of the   2.____

    A. immature personality
    B. psychoneurotic disorder
    C. involutional psychotic reaction
    D. mentally retarded adolescent

3. The mode of psychological adjustment known as regression can BEST be described as   3.____

    A. refusing to think of unpleasant situations
    B. changing to a type of behavior which is characteristic of an earlier period in life
    C. reverting to actions characteristic of an historically early or primitive code of behavior
    D. hostility towards persons or objects that prove frustrating

4. The CHIEF danger in the employment of escape mechanisms as a form of adjustment is that they   4.____

    A. do more harm than good
    B. are socially undesirable
    C. make the experience expensive
    D. leave the basic problem unsolved

5. In essential hypertension, there is a(n)   5.____

    A. *increase* in systolic pressure and a *decrease* in diastolic pressure
    B. *decrease* in systolic pressure and an *increase* in diastolic pressure
    C. *increase* in *both* systolic and diastolic pressure
    D. *decrease* in *both* systolic and diastolic pressure

6. The *initial* paralysis in cerebral vascular accident, regardless of cause, is the type known as   6.____

    A. spastic   B. paraplegic   C. flaccid   D. rigid

7. Cerebral hemorrhage *most frequently* occurs in males in the age range from   7.____

    A. 20 to 30 years   B. 30 to 40 years
    C. 40 to 50 years   D. 50 years and over

8. Hereditary progressive muscular dystrophy is a disease characterized by progressive weakness and final atrophy of groups of muscles.
   Of the following statements about muscular dystrophy, the one which is LEAST accurate is that

   A. there is no known cure for muscular dystrophy at present
   B. muscular dystrophy is a disease of the central nervous system
   C. early signs of muscular dystrophy are frequent falls, difficulty climbing stairs, development of lordosis, and a waddling gait
   D. therapeutic exercises may have some temporary value in the treatment of muscular dystrophy

9. The home care program is an extension of the hospital's service into the home on an extra-mural basis.
   Of the following statements, the one that BEST explains the success of this program is that it

   A. *recognizes* the value to the patient and his family of the preservation of normal family life despite the limitations imposed by the patient's illness
   B. *makes* more hospital beds available for acute illnesses and emergency care
   C. reduces the cost of hospital care by reducing the number of inpatients
   D. *simplifies* hospital administration by reducing the number of chronically ill in hospitals

10. The MOST important of the following reasons for the rehabilitation of the seriously handicapped individual is that

    A. hospitalization of the handicapped is usually prolonged and costly to the community
    B. beds occupied by such patients reduce the number of hospital beds available for acutely ill patients
    C. care of chronically ill or handicapped patients is taxing and difficult for the family, the nurse, and the doctor
    D. it is important to the patient that he be as independent and useful as possible

11. There has been a notable increase in the discharge rate from mental institutions in the state during recent years. This change in statistics may be attributed CHIEFLY to

    A. increasing use of psychoanalysis and better trained personnel
    B. new drugs, changes in admission procedures, and the "open door" policy
    C. the increase in nursing homes for the elderly
    D. the use of psychotherapeutics and early diagnosis of mental illness

12. The PRINCIPAL and BASIC objective of mental hygiene is to

    A. modify attitudes as well as unhealthy behavior secondary to unhealthy attitudes
    B. care for the post-hospitalized psychiatric patient at home
    C. increase mental hygiene clinic services
    D. stimulate interest in improved education for doctors, nurses, and teachers

13. Separation of a child from his own home and placement in a foster home often arouses adverse reactions in the child. Of the following, the one which is MOST serious for the child is

    A. homesickness
    B. withdrawn behavior
    C. rebellion against authority
    D. dislike of new people

14. Behavior problems of the adolescent school child can BEST be explained by the fact that

    A. the adolescent suddenly becomes aware of the opposite sex at this time
    B. the demands made on adolescents by intolerant parents create rebellion against authority
    C. during childhood there is a general disregard of the child's need for independence by parents and other adults
    D. adolescence is a transition period between childhood and adulthood which usually creates feelings of insecurity in the adolescent

15. Of the following, the behavior which is LEAST indicative of serious emotional maladjustment in an adolescent boy is

    A. lying and cheating
    B. shyness and daydreaming
    C. gross overweight
    D. association with a teen-age gang

16. The one of the following diseases which is caused by a birth injury is

    A. cerebral palsy
    B. meningitis
    C. hydrocele
    D. congenital syphilis
    E. epilepsy

17. A delusion is a

    A. disharmony of mind and body
    B. fantastic image formed during sleep
    C. false judgment of objective things
    D. cessation of thought
    E. distorted perception or image

18. The one of the following which is the MOST common form of treatment employed by psychiatrists in treating patients with mental disorders is

    A. hypnotism
    B. hydrotherapy
    C. electroshock
    D. insulin shock
    E. psychotherapy

19. A masochistic person is one who

    A. is very melancholy
    B. has delusions of grandeur about himself
    C. derives pleasure from being cruelly treated
    D. believes in a fatalistic philosophy
    E. derives pleasure from hurting another

20. Surgery is *ESPECIALLY* difficult during the Oedipal period because of the 20.____

    A. father attachment   B. mental age
    C. castration anxieties   D. rejection complex
    E. separation from siblings

21. A psychometric test is one which attempts to measure 21.____

    A. social adjustment   B. emotional maturity
    C. physical activity   D. personality development
    E. Intellectual capacity

22. The one of the following conditions which falls into the classification of a psychosis rather than psychoneurosis is 22.____

    A. anxiety hysteria   B. schizophrenia
    C. neurasthenia   D. convesion hysteria
    E. compulsion neurosis

23. The one of the following which BEST describes psychosomatic medicine is: 23.____

    A. The understanding and treatment of both mind and body in illness
    B. The treatment of disease by psychiatric methods only
    C. The separation of mind and body in medical treatment
    D. The psychological testing of all individuals
    E. A system of socialized medical planning

24. The one of the following conditions for which shock treatment is *FREQUENTLY* used is 24.____

    A. alcoholism   B. Parkinson's syndrome
    C. multiple sclerosis   D. schizophrenia
    E. diabetes

25. The one of the following conditions which is *NOT* caused by the dysfunction of endocrine glands is 25.____

    A. myxedema   B. duodenal ulcer
    C. cretinism   D. Addison's disease
    E. none of the above

KEY (CORRECT ANSWERS)

1.	C	11.	B
2.	B	12.	A
3.	B	13.	B
4.	D	14.	D
5.	C	15.	D
6.	C	16.	A
7.	D	17.	C
8.	B	18.	E
9.	A	19.	C
10.	D	20.	C

21. E
22. B
23. A
24. D
25. B

TEST 2

DIRECTIONS: Each question or incomplete statement is followed by several suggested answers or completions. Select the one that BEST answers the question or completes the statement. *PRINT THE LETTER OF THE CORRECT ANSWER IN THE SPACE AT THE RIGHT.*

1. Euphoria is a state of

   A. depression   B. elation   C. ideation   D. frustration

   1.___

2. An ailment found only in older people is

   A. manic depression
   C. senile dementia
   B. dementia praecox
   D. tabes dorsalis

   2.___

3. The permissive policy employed in some mental hospitals is associated with a(n)

   A. increase in assaultive behavior
   B. open door policy
   C. decrease in the use of physical restraint
   D. increase in the use of physical restraint

   3.___

4. A symptom of dementia praecox is

   A. extroversion
   C. unpredictability
   B. tic paralysis
   D. cerebral hemorrhage

   4.___

5. Substituting an activity in which a person can succeed for one in which he may fail is

   A. sublimation
   C. rationalization
   B. projection
   D. compensation

   5.___

6. Rationalization is the result of

   A. believing what one wants to believe
   B. reflective thinking
   C. scientific thinking
   D. basing conclusions on fact

   6.___

7. Delusions of persecution are typical of

   A. epilepsy
   C. schizophrenia
   B. regression
   D. paranoia

   7.___

8. A person with an IQ of 85 would be classified as

   A. defective
   C. dull average
   B. normal
   D. borderline

   8.___

9. The term describing physical symptoms that do not arise *ENTIRELY* from physical causes is

   A. organic
   C. psychosomatic
   B. psychoneurotic
   D. psychopathological

   9.___

10. The mechanism of attributing one's own ideas to others is termed 10.____

    A. projection B. substitution
    C. sublimation D. rationalization

11. A child's tendency to pattern after his parents is known as 11.____

    A. identification B. projection
    C. compensation D. substitution

12. Stuttering in children USUALLY originates from 12.____

    A. physical handicap B. mentally deficient parents
    C. emotional handicap D. imitation of other stutterers

13. Acute intoxication may PROPERLY be labeled a psychosis because it involves 13.____

    A. intellectual limitations
    B. emotional inadequacies
    C. bodily disease
    D. a severe loss of contact with reality

14. The outstanding change, of the following, in the aging process is that the aged are 14.____

    A. irritable B. no longer self-reliant
    C. senile D. easily influenced by stress

15. Re-adjusting the older person to be somewhat self-sufficient is known as 15.____

    A. stabilization B. regeneration
    C. rejuvenation D. rehabilitation

16. The spastic child usually 16.____

    A. is mentally retarded B. is potentially schizophrenic
    C. requires speech training D. has poor vision

17. Insomnia refers to 17.____

    A. unconsciousness B. sleeplessness
    C. sleep walking D. insensibility

18. A drug recently introduced in the treatment of mental illness is 18.____

    A. streptomycin B. paramino-salicylic acid
    C. reserpine D. cortisone

19. In general, the sleep requirement for an aged person as compared to the sleep requirement for a young adult is 19.____

    A. less B. more C. the same D. slightly greater

20. The MOST IMPORTANT aspect of the rehabilitation of a person who has suffered a stroke is the 20.____

    A. patient's emotional reaction to self
    B. doctor's attitude toward the patient
    C. nurse's attitude toward the patient
    D. family reaction toward the patient

21. If a patient tells a nurse that he is contemplating committing suicide, the nurse should

    A. not pay any attention, since people who threaten suicide seldom follow through
    B. urge him to consult a psychiatrist, since potential suicides need psychiatric help immediately
    C. be sympathetic. Her sympathy will divert him from his intention
    D. realize that he is a neurotic with whom she will try to work

22. The BEST advice you can give parents disturbed by their five-year-old child's habit of nailbiting is to tell them to

    A. find out what some of the pressures on the child are and try to relieve them
    B. paint the child's fingers with the product "bitter aloes"
    C. point out to the child that this is a baby habit and not desirable in a school child
    D. punish the child by not allowing him to watch television or go to the movies

23. In certain periods of development, anti-social behavior in young children is considered normal. However, of the following situations, the one which merits referral to a mental hygiene clinic is where

    A. a two-year-old persists in hitting his four- year-old brother
    B. a three-year-old develops enuresis when a new baby is brought into the home
    C. a four-year-old runs away from home at every opportunity
    D. a six-year-old is not friendly, has no "pals" after six months in school, and participates in activities only when compelled to

24. Learning occurs

    A. when the child's responses are adequate
    B. when a solution to the situation is obvious
    C. when the adult solves the problems
    D. None of the above

25. The FIRST emotions to become differentiated may be described as

    A. anger and fear   B. anger and distress
    C. fear and delight   D. delight and distress

KEY (CORRECT ANSWERS)

1. B
2. C
3. B
4. C
5. D

6. A
7. D
8. C
9. C
10. A

11. A
12. C
13. D
14. D
15. D

16. C
17. B
18. C
19. A
20. A

21. B
22. A
23. D
24. A
25. D

EXAMINATION SECTION
TEST 1

DIRECTIONS: Each question or incomplete statement is followed by several suggested answers or completions. Select the one that BEST answers the question or completes the statement. *PRINT THE LETTER OF THE CORRECT ANSWER IN THE SPACE AT THE RIGHT.*

1. Marked improvement in a child's ability to draw a man over a brief period of time is MOST likely to be related to

    A. better social adjustment
    B. maturational effect
    C. the overcoming of a reading disability
    D. recovery from an illness

2. Phenylketonuria, which is associated with intellectual disability, is a disorder of

    A. the reticuloendothelia system
    B. metabolism
    C. cerebral damage
    D. gyral defect

3. A patient asserts, *I can't stand the agony I suffer when I go against my mother's wishes.* The therapist replies, *You really like to punish that momma inside of you for your dependency, don't you?*
   This response can be viewed as an example of

    A. reassurance   B. interpretation
    C. support   D. reflection of feeling

4. A shy young first grade boy becomes extremely attached to his teacher. He brings her presents, asks her to help him with his clothing a great deal, and wants to sit near her all the time.
   He is MOST likely manifesting the mental mechanism of

    A. introjection   B. sublimation
    C. reaction-formation   D. transference

5. The peculiarities of language behavior in the schizophrenic arise from his extreme need of a feeling of

    A. personal security   B. self-denial
    C. isolation   D. disarticulation

6. The theory that psychical compensation for a feeling of physical or social inferiority is responsible for the development of a psychoneurosis is attributed to

    A. Adler   B. Horney   C. Freud   D. Sullivan

7. Which of the following terms refers to the maintenance of stability in the physiological functioning of the organism?

   A. Functional autonomy B. Canalization
   C. Homeostasis D. Maturation

8. Extensive studies of the personality and behavior of intellectually gifted children generally reveal that they

   A. are physically better developed on the whole than average children
   B. are more likely to be emotionally disturbed than average children
   C. are more prone to divorce in later life than average children
   D. more often come from homes in which emotional disturbance is present

9. Expert opinion of professional workers with the physically handicapped indicates that a list of behavior characteristics would be headed generally by feelings of

   A. aggression B. hostility C. inferiority D. courage

10. Children with pykno-epilepsy suffer from _____ convulsions.

    A. diencephalic B. visceral
    C. psychic equivalent D. no

11. Children with albinism and aniridia may read MOST comfortably with levels of illumination that, in relation to average levels of illumination, are

    A. upper B. middle C. lower D. uneven

12. Phenylpyruvic amentia has been traced to which of the following?

    A. Nutritional deficiency in the prenatal environment
    B. A single recessive gene
    C. Pathological nidation
    D. Effects of radiation

13. Age of mother has been found to be MOST closely associated with the incidence of which of the following?

    A. Cerebral palsy B. Cerebral angiomatosis
    C. Down syndrome D. Hydrocephaly

14. The so-called visual area of the cerebral cortex is located in the _____ lobe.

    A. frontal B. parietal
    C. occipital D. temporal

15. Hypothyroidism is due to _____ in childhood.

    A. thyroid insufficiency B. pituitary insufficiency
    C. thyroid excess D. pituitary excess

16. The inability to express oneself in words in spite of an adequate understanding and imaginal representation is called

    A. agraphia B. aphemia C. agnosia D. aphexia

17. Clara Thompson saw psychoanalysis as a method of therapy primarily designed to 17.____
    A. give the individual new insights into his past experiences
    B. help the individual master his difficulties in living
    C. have the individual re-enact his relationships with his parents
    D. strengthen the individual's ego defenses

18. According to Freud, the source of the large majority of the dreams recorded during analysis is 18.____
    A. a recent and psychologically significant event which is directly represented in the dream
    B. several recent and significant events which are combined by the dream into a single whole
    C. one or more recent and significant events which are represented in the dream-content by allusion to a contemporary but indifferent event
    D. a subjectively significant experience which is constantly represented in the dream by allusion to a recent but indifferent impression

19. When an individual permits unpleasant impulses or thoughts access to consciousness but does not permit their normal elaboration in associative connections and in affect, the psychoanalytic adjustment mechanism involved is 19.____
    A. rationalization   B. conversion
    C. isolation   D. introjection

20. In psychoanalytic thinking, repression can BEST be thought of as a(n) 20.____
    A. attempt in projection
    B. special type of introjection
    C. reflection of acceptance of Id impulses
    D. temporal form of regression

KEY (CORRECT ANSWERS)

1.	A	11.	C
2.	B	12.	B
3.	B	13.	C
4.	D	14.	C
5.	A	15.	A
6.	A	16.	B
7.	C	17.	B
8.	A	18.	D
9.	C	19.	C
10.	D	20.	D

TEST 2

DIRECTIONS: Each question or incomplete statement is followed by several suggested answers or completions. Select the one that BEST answers the question or completes the statement. *PRINT THE LETTER OF THE CORRECT ANSWER IN THE SPACE AT THE RIGHT.*

1. The behavior pattern considered to be deviate by clinicians is

    A. infractions of the moral code
    B. generosity
    C. recessive personality
    D. resistance to authority

2. A symptom of dementia praecox is

    A. tick paralysis
    B. negativism
    C. extroversion
    D. eremophobia

3. According to classic psychoanalytic thinking, the disorder MOST responsive to psychoanalytic therapy is

    A. compulsive neurosis
    B. hysteria
    C. narcissistic neurosis
    D. obsessive neurosis

4. For the therapist, the MOST common meaning of resistance is that it is a(n)

    A. index of lack of suitability for treatment
    B. defensive attempt on the part of the patient
    C. reflection of superior therapeutic promise
    D. relatively rare phenomenon in psychotherapy

5. In a normal distribution, the percentage of children whose IQ's fall between 90 and 110 is APPROXIMATELY

    A. 40   B. 50   C. 60   D. 70

6. The pioneer in mental diseases who was the first to make a distinction between emotional disorder and intellectual disability was

    A. Kraepelin   B. Seguin   C. Esquirol   D. Galton

7. In psychoanalytic thinking, the term superego generally embraces the

    A. necessary social prohibitions as well as the higher cultural strivings and ideals
    B. unconscious strivings of the person as well as the ego-ideal
    C. unconscious reproaches of the person as well as the id strivings
    D. unconscious ego and its defense mechanism as well as the ego-ideal

8. A major contribution of Fromm to psychoanalysis can be considered to be his

    A. attempt to formulate the dynamics of orality and the concept of original sin
    B. belief that man has innate social feeling and a drive for perfection
    C. effort to relate the psychological forces operating in man to the society within which he lives
    D. effort to integrate the concept of psychosexual development with Rankian principles

9. José, a ten-year-old, has a hyperthyroid condition.
It is MOST likely that his behavior will be characterized by

    A. shyness, withdrawal, and reticence
    B. negativism, aggressiveness, and uncooperativeness
    C. placidity, passivity, and psychomotor delays
    D. restlessness, irritability, and excessive activity

10. The etiology of intellectual disability which is attributed to mechanical damage to the fetus would be classified as

    A. exogenous
    B. endogenous
    C. heterogenous
    D. none of the above

11. The majority of children of intellectually disabled parents will have IQ's that in relation to the IQ's of their parents are

    A. somewhat lower
    B. somewhat higher
    C. lower for boys and higher for girls
    D. lower for girls and higher for boys

12. Stuttering and stammering are MOST likely to develop between the ages of _____ years.

    A. 2 and 5
    B. 6 and 9
    C. 10 and 13
    D. 14 and 18

13. Most cases of stuttering are PRIMARILY the result of

    A. changed handedness
    B. hereditary factors
    C. physiological defects
    D. emotional problems

14. Anorexia is a condition which manifests itself in a loss of

    A. vision
    B. appetite
    C. motor control
    D. smell

15. Most differences in play activities and interests between boys and girls in the elementary school years can PROBABLY be attributed to

    A. inherent biological differences
    B. inherent emotional differences
    C. instinctual influences
    D. cultural influences

16. The rate and pattern of early motor development of children depend MAINLY upon

    A. experience
    B. acculturation
    C. maturation
    D. training

17. Of the following, the BEST index of the anatomical age of young children is

    A. brain weight
    B. ossification
    C. basal metabolism
    D. dentition

18. When children of very superior mental ability are compared in size and weight with children of the same age whose mental ability is average, the former children are found to be

    A. above average
    B. average
    C. below average
    D. either above or below average, depending on the age level

18._____

19. The average child speaks his first word at _____ months.

    A. 6   B. 9   C. 12   D. 15

19._____

20. In Pavlov's classical study of conditioning, the unconditioned stimulus was the

    A. food
    B. bell
    C. salivation
    D. electric shock

20._____

21. Contemporary reinforcement learning theory suggests that the MOST effective learning takes place when correct responses are _____ and incorrect responses _____.

    A. rewarded; ignored
    B. rewarded; punished
    C. ignored; punished
    D. none of the above

21._____

22. According to the literature, girls tend to develop physiologically and socially about

    A. the same as boys
    B. one to two years more slowly than boys
    C. one to two years more quickly than boys
    D. none of the above

22._____

23. The mother of a newborn infant is told by her physician that she will have to have corrective surgery performed within the next 2 years. It is expected that the operation in addition to her convalescence will keep her away from her baby approximately one month. The period during which the separation would be LEAST advisable from the standpoint of the child's emotional development is between the ages of _____ months.

    A. 1 and 6
    B. 8 and 16
    C. 16 and 20
    D. 20 and 24

23._____

24. Of the following, the term to which empathy is LEAST related is

    A. sublimation
    B. identification
    C. introjection
    D. projection

24._____

KEY (CORRECT ANSWERS)

1.	C	11.	B
2.	B	12.	A
3.	B	13.	D
4.	B	14.	B
5.	B	15.	D
6.	C	16.	C
7.	A	17.	B
8.	C	18.	A
9.	D	19.	C
10.	A	20.	A

21. A
22. C
23. B
24. A

EXAMINATION SECTION
TEST 1

DIRECTIONS: Each question or incomplete statement is followed by several suggested answers or completions. Select the one that BEST answers the question or completes the statement. *PRINT THE LETTER OF THE CORRECT ANSWER IN THE SPACE AT THE RIGHT.*

1. Epilepsy is MAINLY associated with

    A. brain injury B. migraine
    C. dysrhythmia D. aggressivity

2. A disturbance of language perception and expression is called

    A. aphasia B. amnesia C. amentia D. alexia

3. Alcoholism is MOST commonly connected with

    A. dysrhythmia B. neurosis
    C. psychopathy D. overt homosexuality

4. The polygraph is MOST useful for diagnosing

    A. epilepsy B. aggressivity
    C. deception D. brain damage

5. The electroencephalogram is MOST useful for diagnosing

    A. brain tumor B. epilepsy
    C. brain injury D. mental deficiency

6. Shock therapy was recommended for

    A. paranoid schizophrenics B. depressed psychotics
    C. severe psychoneurotics D. psychopaths

7. Prefrontal lobotomy had been recommended for

    A. aggressive psychotics B. apathetic psychotics
    C. paranoid psychotics D. psychopaths

8. Most authorities believe that mental deficiency is _____ hereditary.

    A. never B. always C. sometimes D. rarely

9. Recent experiments utilizing glutamic acid in an attempt to raise the intellectual level of retarded children have resulted in

    A. inconclusive findings
    B. a marked temporary rise in intellectual level
    C. a marked permanent rise in intellectual level
    D. a slight temporary decline in intellectual level

10. An individual's Rorschach protocol may be MOST profitably interpreted in the light of his

    A. behavior while being tested B. case history
    C. other test results D. presenting problems

11. If a child is mentally retarded, his academic potential can be explained MOST readily to his parent in terms of the status of other children

    A. in his class
    B. of similar CA
    C. of similar MA
    D. of similar IQ

12. It is MOST probable that a school-age child characterized, on the basis of psychological tests, as a mental defective might, in fact, be

    A. epileptic
    B. deaf
    C. mute
    D. schizophrenic

13. The classroom behavior MOST characteristic of the brain injured child includes

    A. distractibility, hyperactivity, and lack of inhibition
    B. listlessness, withdrawal, and compulsiveness
    C. aggressiveness, fearfulness, and egocentrism
    D. perseveration, fatigue, and apathy

14. A child's MOST rapid rate of mental growth generally occurs

    A. during the first few months of life
    B. between the ages of 3-6
    C. between the ages of 6-12
    D. during early adolescence

15. A psychopath may be distinguished by the fact that he commits antisocial acts

    A. consistently
    B. without customary reaction to guilt
    C. without awareness of what he is doing
    D. violently

16. Of the following techniques, the one which is considered to be characteristic of non-directive or client-centered therapy is

    A. encouraging transference
    B. reflection of feeling
    C. free association
    D. permissive questioning

17. Psychoanalytic writers consider the MOST important aspect of an analyst's training to be his

    A. training in psychoanalytic concepts
    B. training in medicine
    C. training in analysis
    D. general psychological training

18. In the transference situation, it is MOST probable that there will be _____ feeling(s) between analyst and patient.

    A. positive
    B. negative
    C. neutral
    D. positive and negative

19. The sequelae of encephalitis   19._____

    A. are now preventable in virtually every case of the disease
    B. may become evident long after an acute attack of the disease
    C. respond readily to treatment when detected
    D. are physical and emotional but rarely mental

20. The mental mechanism most strongly EMPHASIZED in psychoanalytic formulations of   20._____
    schizophrenia is

    A. repression   B. conversion
    C. projection   D. regression

21. Paranoia differs from the paranoid type of schizophrenia in   21._____

    A. the occurrence of delusions in one and not the other
    B. the fact that the paranoid patient does not act on the basis of his delusions
    C. the amount of *psychopathic tainting* in the family history
    D. that the delusions are more systematized

22. According to the Freudian psychoanalysts, the personality changes in general paresis   22._____
    are due to

    A. oedipus complex   B. infantile sex urges
    C. sublimations   D. changes in narcissism

23. A patient who touched his chin when asked to touch his nose would be MOST likely to be   23._____
    suffering from

    A. motor apraxia   B. motor ataxia
    C. sensory apraxia   D. agnosia

24. Shock treatment for schizophrenia, especially by the use of metrazol, was introduced at   24._____
    first because of the theory that

    A. shock arouses special physiological defense mechanisms by way of the *alarm reaction*
    B. shock stimulates the autonomic nervous sytem and thus facilitates homeostasis
    C. convulsions protect epileptics against developing schizophrenic symptoms
    D. shock as a form of punishment gratifies the patient's masochistic tendencies

25. From his survey of experimental evidence on the effect of infant care on later personality,   25._____
    Orlansky was led to the conclusion that such factors as breastfeeding and toilet-training

    A. are of no significance for later personality
    B. are significant determiners of personality
    C. are relevant to personality only insofar as they indicate the mother's attitude, which is the effective factor
    D. may help determine personality but constitutional and post-infantile factors should receive major emphasis

KEY (CORRECT ANSWERS)

1. C
2. A
3. B
4. C
5. B

6. B
7. A
8. C
9. A
10. B

11. C
12. D
13. A
14. A
15. B

16. B
17. C
18. D
19. B
20. D

21. D
22. D
23. A
24. C
25. D

TEST 2

DIRECTIONS: Each question or incomplete statement is followed by several suggested answers or completions. Select the one that BEST answers the question or completes the statement. *PRINT THE LETTER OF THE CORRECT ANSWER IN THE SPACE AT THE RIGHT.*

1. A part of the nervous system NOT known to have any connection with emotional behavior is referred to as the

    A. parasympathetic nervous system
    B. basal ganglia
    C. frontal lobes of cerebral cortex
    D. temporal lobes of cerebral cortex

    1._____

2. A phobia is _____ anxiety.

    A. less specific than
    B. more specific than
    C. synonymous with an
    D. less acute than

    2._____

3. The division of the autonomic nervous system that coordinates bodily changes in fear and anger is

    A. sacral
    B. sympathetic
    C. emergency
    D. cranial

    3._____

4. The effect of familiarity in the case of inter-racial attitudes is

    A. dependent upon the nature of the contact
    B. a tendency to breed contempt
    C. greater understanding and acceptance
    D. of little importance one way or the other

    4._____

5. Negativism is MOST typical of children at the age of _____ year(s).

    A. one   B. three   C. six   D. nine

    5._____

6. Children's groups about the age of two typically show

    A. much cooperation
    B. sex segregation
    C. parallel activity
    D. none of the above

    6._____

7. In which of the following functions does development depend MOST completely upon maturation?

    A. Roller skating
    B. Swimming
    C. Singing
    D. Walking

    7._____

8. In the first months of an infant's life, the baby's reflex responses are

    A. almost the only reactions the baby shows
    B. virtually absent from behavior
    C. more accurate than later in life
    D. less conspicuous than generalized mass reactions

    8._____

9. Play and reading interests of boys and girls will be found to be most DIFFERENT at the age of _____ years.

   A. three   B. six   C. twelve   D. eighteen

10. The unsociability often reported for very bright children is MOST likely to be due to

   A. their biological makeup
   B. their complete absorption in intellectual pursuits
   C. their lack of personal attractiveness
   D. the absence of suitable companions

11. If we measure a number of individuals upon a variety of complex mental functions, we will find that the different functions show _____ relationship.

   A. a negative
   B. no
   C. a fairly high degree of positive
   D. practically a perfect positive

12. Of the following general statements about deterioration in mental patients, which is the MOST questionable at present?

   A. More recently acquired forms of reaction are lost before those formed earlier in life.
   B. Generalization and abstraction in psychoses is qualitatively the same as that in the young child.
   C. Deterioration in many cases regarded as hopeless appears to be reversible.
   D. The responses of a deteriorated person show generally a definite patterning which tends to mask his defects.

13. Concerning the course of intellectual deterioration in the mental disorders, it is CORRECT to state that

   A. defect in the ability to generalize is more characteristic of schizophrenia than of other psychotic states
   B. concept formation deteriorates more slowly in schizophrenia than in senile psychosis
   C. decreased speed and persistence in mental activity are characteristic of epilepsy
   D. senile patients suffer more impairment in the recall of long past events than in recent memory

14. According to mental test comparisons of cooperative patients in the various disease groups, the group which shows the LEAST intellectual impairment is

   A. paranoid schizophrenia   B. psychopathic personality
   C. hebephrenic schizophrenia   D. hysteria

15. Schizophrenic speech is BEST characterized by

   A. loose, approximate use of words and reaction to superficial similarities among ideas and objects
   B. loose, approximate use of words and failure to make use of similarities or analogies

C. unusual amount of stammering and reaction to superficial similarities among ideas and objects
D. unusual amount of stammering and failure to make use of similarities or analogies

16. It is the central, distinguishing feature of the depressive phase of manic-depressive psychosis that the patient   16._____

    A. is keenly aware of lacking a motive for existence
    B. attaches his depression to some irrelevant or imaginary cause
    C. is excessively disturbed over some recent trouble
    D. is overactive, restless, and even agitated

17. In which of the following abilities do dull and gifted children tend to differ most markedly?   17._____

    A. Arithmetical computation
    B. Drawing
    C. Reading comprehension
    D. Spelling

18. The schizophrenic patient is said to exhibit loss of affect. This amounts to   18._____

    A. decreased attention to one's personal feeling tone
    B. lack of emotional reaction toward abstract ideas
    C. increased affectivity to ideas and decreased affectivity concerning persons and events
    D. increased affectiveness in environment but less to abstractions

19. Ability to establish a conditioned response in the eyelid has been found to be a point of differentiation between   19._____

    A. idiopathic epilepsy and hysterical seizures
    B. malingering and traumatic neurosis
    C. senile dementia and cerebral arteriosclerosis
    D. hysterical and organic blindness

20. The MAIN distinction between normal grief and reactive neurosis is in the   20._____

    A. feelings of inadequacy and unreality
    B. lack of basis in real occurrence
    C. duration and intensity of the emotional display
    D. intellectual retardation

21. Kretschmer's dysplastic type applies to those with   21._____

    A. compact, round, fleshy habitus
    B. strong, solid, muscular build
    C. slender bodies, long bones, little muscular strength
    D. conspicuous disharmony due to abnormal functioning of the endocrine glands

22. Which of the following is NOT characteristic of anxiety neurosis? 22.____

    A. Increase of irritable tension
    B. Vague somatic complaints
    C. Hypersensitivity to external stimuli
    D. Temporary muscular paralysis of the limbs

23. Involutional melancholia is usually characterized by a 23.____

    A. marked motor agitation   B. motor depression
    C. flight of ideas   D. loss of affect

24. From our knowledge about hallucinatory phenomena, it can be stated reliably that 24.____

    A. hallucinations occur in association with a dreamlike state
    B. hallucinations and imagery are similar processes differing only in intensity
    C. mescal-induced hallucinations are not similar to schizophrenic hallucinations
    D. organized hallucinations can be produced by direct stimulation of the brain surface

25. Which of the following is NOT a form of epilepsy? 25.____

    A. Grand mal   B. Pyknolepsy
    C. Jacksonian   D. Parkinsonian

KEY (CORRECT ANSWERS)

1. B		11. C	
2. B		12. B	
3. D		13. A	
4. A		14. A	
5. B		15. A	
6. C		16. A	
7. D		17. C	
8. D		18. C	
9. C		19. D	
10. D		20. C	

21. D
22. D
23. A
24. D
25. D

EXAMINATION SECTION
TEST 1

DIRECTIONS: Each question or incomplete statement is followed by several suggested answers or completions. Select the one that BEST answers the question or completes the statement. *PRINT THE LETTER OF THE CORRECT ANSWER IN THE SPACE AT THE RIGHT.*

1. A patient tells you that the other patients are plotting to kill him. This is MOST likely an example of

    A. a manic-depressive reaction
    B. a paranoid reaction
    C. excellent perceptual skills on the part of the patient
    D. a compulsive reaction

2. Which of the following statements is TRUE?

    A. Diagnoses are, by their very nature, always accurate.
    B. Phobic reactions are the most common reasons people are admitted to mental hospitals.
    C. People with neuroses are far less likely to be hospitalized than people with psychoses.
    D. Severely depressed patients are less of a suicide risk than any other patient group, except paranoid schizophrenics.

3. The LARGEST single diagnostic group of psychotic patients are

    A. neurotic depressive
    B. schizophrenic
    C. obsessive-compulsive
    D. paranoid reactive

4. The personality type that would BEST be characterized by the description that *he or she has no conscience* would be the

    A. drug addict
    B. exhibitionist
    C. sociopath
    D. manic-depressive

5. Of the following, the marked inability to organize one's thoughts is found MOST commonly and severely in

    A. schizophrenics
    B. amnesiacs
    C. those suffering from anxiety neuroses
    D. sociopaths

6. Someone who constantly feels tense, anxious, and worried but is unable to identify exactly why is MOST likely to be suffering from

    A. anxiety neurosis
    B. schizophrenia
    C. dissociative reaction
    D. a conversion reaction

7. A patient always insists upon twirling around six times before entering a new room, or she fears she will die. This is an example of

    A. paranoid reaction
    B. obsessive-compulsive reaction
    C. dissociative reaction
    D. anxiety neurosis

8. Of the following, those who suffer from neuroses would USUALLY complain of 8.____

    A. rejections, dissociation, and frequent inability to remember what day it is
    B. delusions, rejections, and feeling tired
    C. tiredness, fears, and hallucinations
    D. fears, physical complaints, and anxieties

9. The category that is caused by a disorder of the brain for which physical pathology can be demonstrated is 9.____

    A. neurotic depressive reaction   B. schizophrenia
    C. functional psychoses   D. organic psychoses

10. Of the following, which is NOT true? 10.____

    A. Someone who is suddenly unable to hear for psychological reasons would be considered to be suffering from a conversion reaction.
    B. If someone is in fugue, they have combined amnesia with flight.
    C. *Multiple personalities* is a dissociative reaction that affects primarily the elderly.
    D. General symptoms of schizophrenia include an ability to deal with reality, the presence of delusions or hallucinations, and inappropriate affect.

11. Which one of the following is TRUE? 11.____

    A. Calling an elderly person *gramps* or *granny* makes them feel more secure.
    B. It is important for an elderly person to maintain his or her independence whenever possible.
    C. When elderly patients start acting like children, they should be treated like children.
    D. It is important to encourage the elderly to hurry because they tend to move so slowly.

12. It has been found that older patients learn BEST when one does all but which one of the following? 12.____

    A. Allowing plenty of time for them to practice and learn
    B. Creating a relaxing environment for them
    C. Dealing with one thing at a time
    D. Assuming little knowledge on their part

13. Which of the following contains the main factors that should be considered before administering medications to elderly patients? 13.____

    A. How popular the medication is with the patient and the team leader's recommendations
    B. Any organic brain damage, liver dysfunction, and body weight
    C. Liver dysfunction, the patient's medical history, and decreased body weight
    D. Decreased body weight, impaired circulation, liver dysfunction, and increased sensitivity to medications

14. When communicating with the hearing impaired, it is BEST to do all of the following EXCEPT

    A. make sure the person can see your lips
    B. speak slowly and clearly
    C. use gestures
    D. shout

15. The three most common visual disorders in the elderly are cataracts, diabetic retinopathy, and glaucoma.
    Of the following statements about these, the one that is NOT true is that

    A. the symptoms for cataracts are a need for brighter light and a need to hold things very near the eyes
    B. diabetic retinopathy, if untreated, can cause blindness, so any vision or eye problems in diabetics should be promptly reported
    C. glaucoma develops slowly, so it is much easier to detect than cataracts or diabetic retinopathy
    D. some of the symptoms of glaucoma are loss of vision out of the corner of the eye, headaches, nausea, eye pain, tearing, blurred vision, and halos around objects of light

16. Which of the following is NOT true?

    A. Most of the elderly hospitalized for psychiatric problems suffer from senile brain atrophy or brain changes that occur due to arteriosclerosis.
    B. It is important to allow the elderly who wish to, the right to always live in the past.
    C. The majority of the elderly are competent, alert, and functioning well in their communities.
    D. Many elderly patients feel that they are no longer valued members of our society.

17. Of the following, which is NOT a good reason for helping the elderly patient stay active? Activity

    A. promotes good health by stimulating appetite and regulating bowel function
    B. prevents the complications of inactivity such as pneumonia, bed sores, and joint immobility
    C. can create an interest in taking more medication
    D. can increase blood circulation

18. Staff members must come to an understanding of their own feelings about the elderly because

    A. the staff may then be more helpful
    B. any negative feelings one has may be difficult to hide
    C. feelings of fear or aversion can be easily transmitted
    D. all of the above

19. An elderly patient will probably eat better if

    A. food servings are large
    B. the foods are chewy
    C. he or she is allowed to finish his/her meals at a leisurely pace
    D. cooked food is served cold

20. The MOST common accident to the elderly involves

    A. falls   B. burns   C. bruises   D. cuts

21. Which of the following is TRUE?

    A. Children should be considered and treated as miniature adults.
    B. Children are growing, developing human beings who will react to situations according to their level of development and the experiences to which they have been subjected.
    C. Children who are brought to a mental health center are usually calm and non-apprehensive on their first visit.
    D. The problems of adolescents are usually overestimated.

22. In working with adolescents, it would be BEST to

    A. neither bend over backwards to give in to demands, nor control them by rigid and punitive means
    B. dress the way most adolescents do
    C. staff those units with young people
    D. watch television with them regularly

23. Of the following, when working with children, it is MOST important to be

    A. consistent
    B. strict
    C. more concerned for their welfare than for the welfare of the other patients
    D. well-liked

24. Of the following, the element that is MOST lacking in relationships between adolescents and adults is

    A. respect   B. fear   C. trust   D. sensitivity

25. Of the following, the BEST reason for grouping children together would be

    A. they should be protected from the influences of all adult patients
    B. children tend to feel more comfortable with other children
    C. children are less likely to *act out* when they are with other children
    D. they would be unable to bother adult patients

26. All of the following statements are true EXCEPT:
    A. Accidents, reactions to drugs, fevers, and disease may each contribute to mental or emotional problems
    B. How effectively an individual reacts to and manages stress contributes to his or her mental health
    C. There is significant research that indicates that mental illness is caused primarily by genetic transmittal
    D. A person's upbringing, his or her relationships with family or friends, past experiences, and present living conditions may all contribute to the status of his or her mental health

27. All of the following are basic psychological needs which must be met for a person to have self-esteem EXCEPT
    A. acceptance and understanding
    B. trust, respect, and security
    C. a rewarding romantic relationship
    D. pleasant interactions with other people

28. All of the following statements are true EXCEPT:
    A. Most people become mentally ill because they are unable to cope with or adapt to the stresses and problems of life
    B. People with emotional problems can rarely be helped enough to live independently
    C. Most of the diseases and symptoms of the body which plague people have a large emotional component as their cause
    D. Environmental and familial factors are more important than genetic factors in mental illness

29. The following are all optimal aspects of family functioning EXCEPT
    A. communication is open and direct
    B. expression of emotion is more often positive than negative
    C. minor problems are ignored, knowing they will go away on their own
    D. there is a high degree of congruence or harmony between the family's values and the actual realities of the society

30. All of the following statements are true EXCEPT:
    A. People who are wealthy rarely become mentally ill
    B. Physical disease may influence emotional balance
    C. People who are mentally ill are often very sensitive to what is happening in their environment
    D. Most people doubt their own sanity at one time or another

31. All of the following statements are true EXCEPT:
    A. Hereditary factors are not the primary cause of mental illness
    B. A person may react to an extremely traumatic experience by becoming mentally ill
    C. Early recognition and treatment does not affect the course of mental illness
    D. Mental illness can develop suddenly

32. All of the following statements are true EXCEPT:

    A. Emotionally disturbed people are usually very sensitive to how other people feel towards them
    B. People do not inherit mental disorders, but may inherit a predisposition to certain types of mental problems
    C. There are many factors which can cause mental illness
    D. Mood swings are signs of mental illness

33. Which of the following statements is LEAST accurate?

    A. The difference between being mentally healthy and mentally ill often lies in the intensity and frequency of inappropriate behavior.
    B. The way a person views a situation determines his or her response to the situation.
    C. The mentally ill are permanently disabled.
    D. Different personal experiences cause a difference in what a person perceives as stressful, and how much stress a person can tolerate.

34. All of the following statements are true EXCEPT:

    A. Most experts in the field of mental health believe that the experiences which occur during the first twenty, or the first six, years of life are the most significant
    B. An unfortunate characteristic of children is that they tend to blame themselves for failures of their parents, and thus may develop feelings of inadequacy which may affect them all of their lives
    C. If neglect is severe enough, an infant or young child may withdraw from reality into a fantasy world which feels less threatening
    D. Human beings develop in the exact same pattern and almost at the same rate

35. Schizophrenia is

    A. genetically caused
    B. most often caused by the habitual use of drugs
    C. the result of a complex relationship between biological, psychological, and sociological factors
    D. most commonly caused by the inhalation of toxic gases

KEY (CORRECT ANSWERS)

1.	B	16.	B
2.	C	17.	C
3.	B	18.	D
4.	C	19.	C
5.	A	20.	A
6.	A	21.	B
7.	B	22.	A
8.	D	23.	A
9.	D	24.	C
10.	C	25.	B
11.	B	26.	C
12.	D	27.	C
13.	D	28.	B
14.	D	29.	C
15.	C	30.	A

31. C
32. D
33. C
34. D
35. C

TEST 2

DIRECTIONS: Each question or incomplete statement is followed by several suggested answers or completions. Select the one that BEST answers the question or completes the statement. *PRINT THE LETTER OF THE CORRECT ANSWER IN THE SPACE AT THE RIGHT.*

1. Tardive dyskenesia is a(n)

    A. antidepressant
    B. birth-related serious injury
    C. serious side effect of phenothiazine derivatives
    D. antiparkinsons drug

2. People taking psychotropic drugs are MOST likely to be sensitive to

    A. long exposures to sunlight
    B. darkness
    C. noise
    D. other patients

3. An antipsychotic drug that is a phenothiazine derivative would MOST likely be used for

    A. helping a patient lose weight
    B. calming a patient
    C. helping a patient sleep
    D. reducing the frequency of delusions in a patient

4. Of the following, an antidepressant such as Elavil would MOST likely be used for

    A. the immediate prevention of suicidal action in a newly admitted patient
    B. helping a patient lose weight
    C. elevating a patient's mood
    D. diuretic purposes

5. Which of the following statements is NOT true?

    A. Antianxiety tranquilizers such as sparine, librium, and vistaril are useful primarily with psychoneurotic and psychosomatic disorders.
    B. Minor or antianxiety tranquilizers tend to be less habit-forming than major or antipsychotic tranquilizers.
    C. Akinesia, pseudoparkinsonism, and tardive dyskenesia are serious side effects of antipsychotic drugs, or phenothiazine derivatives.
    D. Generally, those using tranquilizers like sparine or librium are in less danger of deadly drug overdoses than those using barbituates.

6. All of the following statements are false EXCEPT:

    A. Antipsychotic drugs promote increased sexual interest
    B. Patients no longer need to take their medication when they feel better
    C. Phenothiazines are psychotropic drugs
    D. One of the main difficulties with antipsychotic drugs is that they tend to be habit-forming

7. Yellowing of the skin or eyes, sensitivity to light and pseudoparkinsonism may occur in patients receiving

   A. mellaril or thorazine
   B. librium or tranxene
   C. valium or vistaril
   D. antiparkinson drugs

8. Which of the following is NOT true of extrapyramidal symptoms (EPS)? They

   A. may appear after many weeks of use of phenothiazines
   B. can safely be controlled without medical assistance
   C. may appear after the patient has been taking the drug for only a few days
   D. may include pseudoparkinsonism

9. The time required to reach an effective blood level for an antidepressant medication would MOST likely be three

   A. days   B. hours   C. weeks   D. months

10. An example of a psychotropic drug would be

    A. seconal   B. aspirin   C. librium   D. perichloz

11. In evaluating a patient you are meeting for the first time, it would be best NOT to

    A. be as objective as possible
    B. question one's own motives and reactions when processing data during and after the meeting
    C. be extremely goal-oriented
    D. not allow any praise or criticism directed at you by the patient to influence your assessment

12. All of the following statements are true EXCEPT:

    A. People communicate non-verbally via their behavior and their body posture
    B. Non-verbal clues may be a better indication of a patient's true feelings than what the patient actually says
    C. A patient who is highly anxious is easier to evaluate than a patient who is relatively calm
    D. People should be judged objectively

13. When asking a patient a question, one should do all of the following EXCEPT

    A. phrase questions in order to receive a yes or no response
    B. ask only relevant questions
    C. listen carefully to the response before asking the next question
    D. phrase questions clearly

14. The MAIN purpose for extensive record keeping is to

    A. provide an accurate description of the patient's diagnosis
    B. provide a subjective report of the patient's behavior
    C. provide an objective report of the patient's behavior
    D. give mental health personnel something to do

15. When talking to a patient for the first time, one must realize that

   A. hostile behavior indicates an extremely severe disorder in the patient
   B. a patient's physical appearance will indicate how successful you will be in communicating with the patient
   C. the patient is extremely nervous
   D. you are both strangers to each other

16. Of the following, which statement is NOT true?

   A. The rapid assessment of a patient is not necessarily accomplished by asking a series of routine questions.
   B. There is value, in assessing a patient, in creating a conversational bridge which has *here and now* relevance.
   C. One can assess a patient's state by his or her reaction to a warm greeting given to him or her.
   D. There is some value in routinely asking certain questions, when needed, in order to check a patient's orientation and memory.

17. All of the following could be signs that someone is moving towards mental illness EXCEPT

   A. exhibiting a degree of prolonged, constant anxiety, apprehension, or fear which is out of proportion with reality
   B. severe appetite disturbances
   C. occasional depression
   D. abrupt changes in a person's behavior

18. The first few minutes of interaction with a patient can reveal all but

   A. a patient's contact with reality
   B. whether you are comfortable with a patient
   C. a patient's mood
   D. a patient's chances for recovery

19. Which of the following statements is TRUE?

   A. The tentative diagnosis made when a patient is first admitted is the most accurate diagnosis.
   B. One should always try and keep in mind the state the patient was in when first admitted.
   C. A diagnosis is actually an ongoing process.
   D. When assessing patients' behavior, it is best to be suspicious of what may look like progress.

20. All of the following are examples of defense mechanisms EXCEPT

   A. projection
   B. complimenting someone
   C. displacement
   D. regression

21. A treatment plan is likely to be MOST effective if the

   A. patient's suggestions are always incorporated
   B. patient is voluntarily and wholeheartedly participating in the treatment plan designed for him or her

C. patient has daily contact with his or her family
D. patient respects the team leader

22. All of the following are true EXCEPT:

    A. Patients do not become well simply by people doing something for them
    B. A patient's well-being is enhanced when one or more team members can forge a *therapeutic alliance* with that patient
    C. The most important purpose of the treatment team is to administer the proper medications to patients
    D. It is important that a patient be seen as an individual, and not just as a *case* or a *number*

23. Of the following, a member of the treatment team can BEST assist a patient by

    A. commanding respect from other team members
    B. carefully observing the behavior of patients
    C. avoiding spending too much time with patients
    D. becoming friends with a patient

24. Of the following, which is LEAST important when considering a treatment plan?

    A. Involving the patient
    B. Setting reasonable goals
    C. Being as specific as possible in setting completion dates for goals, and sticking to them
    D. Detailing the methods to be followed, and the work assignments

25. All of the following are true EXCEPT:

    A. A treatment team should help patients understand that they can improve their condition if they will cooperate with the treatment plan
    B. Patients should be encouraged to participate in the programs designed for them
    C. Patients should be encouraged to revise their treatment plans
    D. One's approach should be tailored for each individual, whenever possible

26. All of the following could be considered appropriate goals for patients to work towards, EXCEPT to

    A. expand one's capacity to find or create acceptable options
    B. learn to be less dependent
    C. give up feeling persecuted
    D. learn how to get what one needs, at any cost

27. In working in treatment teams, it is MOST important for team members to

    A. communicate effectively with each other
    B. enjoy working with each other
    C. keep morale high
    D. attend meetings on time

28. One of the purposes of the treatment team is to

    A. decrease the amount of work
    B. coordinate and integrate services to patients
    C. provide training
    D. provide patients with basic counseling skills they can use

29. When working with someone exhibiting a manic-depressive psychosis, depressed type, it is BEST to

    A. concern yourself primarily with his or her eating habits
    B. focus primarily on their sleeping habits
    C. take every statement he or she may make about suicide seriously
    D. allow them to watch a great deal of television

30. In working with a paranoid patient, all of the following are true EXCEPT:
    It

    A. is important to listen with respect
    B. is helpful to establish a trusting relationship
    C. is good to try and talk the patient out of his or her fears
    D. would not be a good practice to agree with their statements, if they are not true

31. It is important, when dealing with verbally abusive patients, to keep in mind all of the following EXCEPT:

    A. Patients usually become abusive because of frustrating circumstances beyond their control
    B. In most cases, the patients do not mean anything personal by their abusive remarks; they are displacing anger
    C. It is important for staff members to remain calm and controlled when patients have emotional outbursts
    D. It is a good idea to allow an angry patient to draw you into an argument, as this will eventually help calm him or her down

32. When dealing with a patient who insists upon doing a number of rituals before brushing his teeth, it would be BEST to

    A. attempt to tease him out of his behavior
    B. not be critical of the ritualistic behavior
    C. perform the same rituals so that he feels more secure
    D. insist that he eliminate one step of the ritual each week

33. A patient tells you that he is balancing an automobile on the top of his head, and asks you what you think of that.
    An APPROPRIATE response for you to make would be:

    A. to ask him to take you for a ride
    B. *Stop saying ridiculous things*
    C. *I know you believe you are balancing a car on your head but I don't see it, therefore I have to assume that you're not*
    D. *Is it an invisible car*

34. A new patient, who is very paranoid, refuses to take off his clothes before getting into bed.
Which would be MOST helpful?

   A. Getting another staff member to assist in removing his clothes
   B. Leaving the room until he comes to his senses
   C. Trying to find out why the patient does not want to undress
   D. Allowing the patient to stay up all night

35. In handling depressed patients, it is BEST to

   A. encourage them to participate in activities
   B. remind them often that things will be better tomorrow
   C. remember that depressed patients have few feelings of guilt
   D. let them know that you know just how they are feeling

36. A patient tells you that she is very depressed over the recent death of her brother.
Which of the following would be the MOST appropriate response?

   A. *Everybody gets depressed when they lose someone they love.*
   B. *It could have been worse; at least he was ill only a short time.*
   C. *I know just how you feel.*
   D. *This must be very difficult for you.*

37. A patient who recently suffered a stroke refuses to let you help her bathe.
This is probably because

   A. it is hard for her to accept that she can no longer do things for herself that she could do before the stroke
   B. she does not like you
   C. she is extremely independent and should be encouraged to be less so
   D. you need to review your methods for bathing patients

38. All of the following would be appropriate in working with a patient who is hallucinating EXCEPT

   A. carefully watch what you are non-verbally communicating
   B. ask concrete, reality-oriented questions
   C. provide a calm, structured environment
   D. agree with the patient, if asked, that you are experiencing the same state he or she is

39. In dealing with overactive patients, it is BEST to

   A. not give most of your attention to these patients, leaving the quieter patients to look after themselves
   B. keep in mind that overactive patients are always more interesting than other patients
   C. remember that overactive patients need more care than other patients
   D. forcibly restrain them whenever possible

40. A patient with mild organic brain damage is very withdrawn and negativistic. 40.____
    The BEST approach, of the following, would be
    A. I need a partner to play cards with me
    B. Your family is very disappointed in you when you act like this
    C. Your doctor said you should participate in all activities here, so you'd better do that
    D. Would you like to go to your room so you can be alone?

KEY (CORRECT ANSWERS)

1. C	11. C	21. B	31. D
2. A	12. C	22. C	32. B
3. D	13. A	23. B	33. C
4. C	14. C	24. C	34. C
5. B	15. D	25. C	35. A
6. C	16. C	26. D	36. D
7. A	17. C	27. A	37. A
8. B	18. D	28. B	38. D
9. C	19. C	29. C	39. A
10. C	20. B	30. C	40. A

EXAMINATION SECTION
TEST 1

DIRECTIONS: Each question or incomplete statement is followed by several suggested answers or completions. Select the one that BEST answers the question or completes the statement. *PRINT THE LETTER OF THE CORRECT ANSWER IN THE SPACE AT THE RIGHT.*

1. In reporting on a person who thinks he sees objects which are NOT present and may NOT be real, the assistant should describe such an individual as having

   A. claustrophobia B. delusions
   C. hallucinations D. paranoia

   1.____

2. An adolescent who is habitually discontented could BEST be described as

   A. invidious B. plaintive
   C. quibbling D. captious

   2.____

3. Occupational therapy is MOST closely associated with

   A. vocational guidance B. position classification
   C. curative handicraft D. diathermic treatment

   3.____

4. Of the following degrees of deviation from normal mentality, the one indicating the LEAST intelligence is the

   A. moron B. imbecile C. idiot D. borderline

   4.____

5. The person whose duty it is to manage the estate of a minor or of an incompetent is called the

   A. executor B. probate officer
   C. amicus curiae D. guardian

   5.____

6. *"Ostensibly a sane person, yet severely mentally ill and dangerous to himself and others,"* is a description MOST commonly applied to a

   A. psychopath B. paraplegic C. paretic D. paranoid

   6.____

7. The impact upon society of mental disease is MOST adequately indicated by

   A. its responsibility for sex crimes and delinquency
   B. the phenomenal growth of feeble-mindedness in the United States
   C. the increasing number of deaths resulting from it
   D. the burden of its disabling effects on the community

   7.____

8. A deficiency disease is a disorder caused by a(n)

   A. deficiency of medical aid
   B. diet lacking certain vitamins or minerals
   C. lack of proper rest and relaxation
   D. insufficient quantity of sugar in the diet

   8.____

9. Delinquency on the part of a child is believed to result PRIMARILY from   9._____
   A. emotional and personality maladjustments
   B. environmental handicaps
   C. physical disability
   D. sociological factors

10. Current interst in child guidance clinics was developed because of an increasing belief that   10._____
    A. at least one-tenth of the nation's youth is destined to end in prison if not given systematic guidance
    B. children should be treated as miniature adults
    C. many of the emotional and mental disabilities of later life result from unfortunate childhood experiences
    D. the best interests of the nation require standardization of each child's education

11. *"The fundamental desires for food, shelter, family and approval, and their accompanying instinctive forms of behavior, are among the most important forces in human life because they are essential to and directly connected with the preservation and the welfare of the individual as well as of the race."*   11._____
    According to this statement
    A. as long as human beings are permitted to act instinctively they will act wisely
    B. the instinct for self-preservation makes the individual consider his own welfare rather than that of others
    C. racial and individual welfare depend upon the fundamental desires
    D. the preservation of the race demands that instinctive behavior be modified

12. *"The growth of our cities, the increasing tendency to move from one part of the country to another, the existence of people of different cultures in the neighborhood, have together made it more and more difficult to secure group recreation as part of informal family and neighborhood life."*   12._____
    According to this statement,
    A. the breaking up of family and neighborhood ties discourages new family and neighborhood group recreation
    B. neighborhood recreation no longer forms a significant part of the larger community
    C. the growth of cities crowds out the development of all recreational activities
    D. the non-English speaking people do not accept new activities easily

13. *"Sublimation consists in directing some inner urge, arising from a lower psychological level, into some channel of interest on a higher psychological level. Pugnaciousness, for example, is directed into some athletic activity involving combat, such as football or boxing, where rules of fair play and the ethics of the game lift the destructive urge for combat into a constructive experience and offer opportunities for the development of character and personality."*   13._____
    According to this statement,
    A. the manner of self-expression may be directed into constructive activities
    B. athletic activities such as football and boxing are destructive of character

C. all conscious behavior on high psychological levels indicates the process of sublimation
D. the rules of fair play are inconsistent with pugnaciousness

14. The one of the following statements which can MOST conceivably be characterized as true is:

    A. Generally speaking, the younger a person is, the less easily he can be influenced by suggestion.
    B. If a therapy assistant has sufficient technical knowledge of his duties, it is not necessary for him to exercise tact in dealing with patients.
    C. A therapy assistant should reject entirely hearsay evidence in making a social diagnosis of a case.
    D. One of the characteristics of adolescence is a feeling in the child that he is misunderstood.

15. The statement that those parental attitudes are good which offer emotional security to the child BEST expresses the notion that

    A. emotionally secure children do not have feelings of aggression
    B. children should not be held accountable for their actions
    C. parental attitudes are inadequate which do not give the child feelings of belonging and freedom for experience
    D. a family in which there is economic dependence cannot be good for the child

16. When advised of the need for medical treatment over an extended period of time in a locality some distance from home, the parent of a child with a cardiac ailment decide to send him to a home in another town. The BEST home for the child in this town would be one

    A. in which there are already residing two foster children who require rest and quiet
    B. in which the family is on relief
    C. in which there are two active boys of the same age as this child
    D. with the bathroom and bedroom on the second floor

17. In planning for the vocational rehabilitation of a physically handicapped person, the use of the sheltered workshop can be a very helpful resource.
    Of the following, the client for whom such service would be MOST appropriate is the one who

    A. will need a constructive way to spend his time for an indefinite period
    B. because of advanced age, is unable to compete in the labor market
    C. needs a transitional experience between his medical care and undertaking a regular job
    D. has a handicap which permanently precludes any gainful employment

18. A group counseling service to parents focused on the understanding of child development and parent-child relations is available through

    A. Childville
    B. The Arthur Lehman Counseling Service
    C. The State Association for Mental Health
    D. The Child Study Association of America

19. A patient is being discharged from an institutional setting following an initial diagnosis and stabilizing treatment for a diabetic condition of which he had not been aware. His doctor recommends a diet and medication regime for the patient to follow at home, but the patient is uncertain about his ability to carry this out on his own.
A community resource that might be MOST helpful in such a situation is a

    A. visiting nurse service
    B. homemaker service
    C. neighborhood health center
    D. dietitian's service

20. "Experience pragmatically suggests that dislocation from cultural roots and customs makes for tension, insecurity, and anxiety. This holds for the child as well as the adolescent, for the new immigrant as well as the second-generation citizen."
Of the following, the MOST important implication of the above statement is that

    A. anxiety, distress and incapacity are always personal and can be understood best only through an understanding of the child's peresent cultural environment
    B. in order to resolve the conflicts caused by the displacement of a child from a home with one cultural background to one with another, it is essential that the child fully replace his old culture with the new one
    C. no treatment goal can be envisaged for a dislocated child which does not involve a value judgment which is itself culturally determined
    D. anxiety and distress result from a child's reaction to culturally oriented treatment goals

21. Accepting the fact that mentally gifted children represent superior heredity, the United States faces an important eugenic problem CHIEFLY because

    A. unless these mentally gifted children mature and reproduce more rapidly than the less intelligent children, the nation is heading for a lowering of the average intelligence of its people
    B. although the mentally gifted child always excels scholastically, he generally has less physical stamina than the normal child and tends to lower the nation's population physically
    C. the mentally subnormal are increasing more rapidly than the mentally gifted in America, thus affecting the overall level of achievement of the gifted child
    D. unless the mental level of the general population is raised to that of the gifted child, the mentally gifted will eventually usurp the reigns of government and dominate the mentally weaker

22. The form of psychiatric treatment which requires the LEAST amount of participation on the part of the patient is

    A. psychoanalysis   B. psychotherapy
    C. shock therapy   D. non-directive therapy

23. Tests administered by psychologists for the PRIMARY purpose of measuring intelligence are known as _____ tests.

    A. protective   B. validating
    C. psychometric   D. apperception

24. In recent years there have been some significant changes in the treatment of patients in state psychiatric hospitals. These changes are PRIMARILY caused by the use of

   A. electric shock therapy
   B. tranquilizing drugs
   C. steroids
   D. the open ward policy

25. The psychological test which makes use of a set of 20 pictures each depicting a dramatic scene is known as the

   A. Goodenough Test
   B. Thematic Apperception Test
   C. Minnesota Multiphasic Personality Inventory
   D. Healy Picture Completion Test

26. One of the MOST effective ways in which experimental psychologists have been able to study the effects on personality of heredity and environment has been through the study of

   A. primitive cultures
   B. identical twins
   C. mental defectives
   D. newborn infants

27. In hospitals with psychiatric divisions, the psychiatric function is predominantly that of

   A. the training of personnel in all psychiatric disciplines
   B. protection of the community against potentially dangerous psychiatric patients
   C. research and study of psychiatric patients so that new knowledge and information can be made generally available
   D. short-term hospitalization designed to determine diagnosis and recommendations for treatment

28. Predictions of human behavior on the basis of past behavior frequently are inaccurate because

   A. basic patterns of human behavior are in a continual state of flux
   B. human behavior is not susceptible to explanation of a scientific nature
   C. the underlying psychological mechanisms of behavior are not completely understood
   D. quantitative techniques for the measurement of stimuli and responses are unavailable

29. Socio-cultural factors are being re-evaluated in casework practice as they influence both the worker and the client in their participation in the casework process.
Of the following factors, the one which is currently being studied MOST widely is the

   A. social class of worker and client and its significance in casework
   B. difference in native intelligence which can be ascribed to racial origin of an individual
   C. cultural values affecting the areas in which an individual functions
   D. necessity in casework treatment of the client's membership in an organized religious group

30. Deviant behavior is a sociological term used to describe behavior which is not in accord with generally accepted standards. This may include juvenile delinquency, adult criminality, mental or physical illness. Comparison of normal with deviant behavior is useful because it

    A. makes it possible to establish watertight behavioral descriptions
    B. provides evidence of differential social behavior which distinguishes deviant from normal behavior
    C. indicates that deviant behavior is of no concern to caseworkers
    D. provides no evidence that social role is a determinant of behavior

31. Alcoholism may affect an individual client's ability to function as a spouse, parent, worker and citizen. Your responsibility to a client with a history of alcoholism is to

    A. interpret to the client the causes of alcoholism as a disease syndrome
    B. work with the alcoholic's family to accept him as he is and to stop trying to reform him
    C. encourage the family of the alcoholic to accept treatment
    D. determine the origins of his particular drinking problem, establish a diagnosis, and work out a treatment plan for him

32. There is a trend to regard narcotic addiction as a form of illness for which the current methods of intervention have not been effective. Research on the combination of social, psychological and physical causes of addiction would indicate that social workers should

    A. oppose hospitalization of addicts in institutions
    B. encourage the addict to live normally at home
    C. recognize that there is no successful treatment for addiction and act accordingly
    D. use the existing community facilities differentially for each addict

33. A study of social relationships among delinquent and non-delinquent youth has shown that

    A. delinquent youths generally conceal their true feelings and maintain furtive contacts
    B. delinquents are more impulsive and vivacious than law-abiding boys
    C. non-delinquent youths diminish their active social relationships in order to sublimate any anti-social impulses
    D. delinquent and non-delinquent youths exhibit similar characteristics of impulsiveness and vivaciousness

34. The one of the following which is the CHIEF danger of interpreting the delinquent behavior of a child in terms of morality alone when attempting to get at its causes is that

    A. this tends to overlook the likelihood that the causes of the child's actions are more than a negation of morality and involve varied symptoms of disturbance
    B. a child's moral outlook toward life and society is largely colored by that of his parents, thus encouraging parent-child conflicts
    C. too careful a consideration of the moral aspects of the offense and of the child's needs may often negate the demands of justice in a case
    D. standards of morality may be of no concern to the delinquent and he may not realize the seriousness of his offenses

35. An adult with a mental age of 9 years is regarded psychologically as 35._____

    A. of normal mentality   B. a moron
    C. an imbecile   D. an idiot

KEY (CORRECT ANSWERS)

1.	C	16.	A
2.	B	17.	C
3.	C	18.	D
4.	C	19.	A
5.	D	20.	C
6.	A	21.	A
7.	D	22.	C
8.	B	23.	C
9.	A	24.	B
10.	C	25.	B
11.	C	26.	B
12.	A	27.	D
13.	A	28.	C
14.	D	29.	C
15.	C	30.	B

31. D
32. D
33. B
34. A
35. B

EXAMINATION SECTION
TEST 1

DIRECTIONS: Each question or incomplete statement is followed by several suggested answers or completions. Select the one that BEST answers the question or completes the Statement. *PRINT THE LETTER OF THE CORRECT ANSWER IN THE SPACE AT THE RIGHT.*

Questions 1-5.

DIRECTIONS: Answer questions 1 through 5 on the basis of the following passage.

Mental disorders are found in a fairly large number of the inmates in correctional institutions. There are no exact figures as to the inmates who are mentally disturbed -- partly because it is hard to draw a precise line between "mental disturbance" and "normality" -- but experts find that somewhere between 15% and 25% of inmates are suffering from disorders that are obvious enough to show up in routine psychiatric examinations. Society has not yet really come to grips with the problem of what to do with mentally disturbed offenders. There is not enough money available to set up treatment programs for all the people identified as mentally disturbed; and there would probably not be enough qualified psychiatric personnel available to run such programs even if they could be set up. Most mentally disturbed offenders are therefore left to serve out their time in correctional institutions, and the burden of dealing with them falls on correction officers. This means that a correction ofcer must be sensitive enough to human behavior to know when he is dealing with a person who is not mentally normal, and that the officer must be imaginative enough to be able to sense how an abnormal individual might react under certain circumstances.

1. According to the above passage, mentally disturbed inmakes in correctional institutions

   A. are usually transferred to mental hospitals when their condition is noticed
   B. cannot be told from other inmates, because tests cannot distinguish between insane people and normal people
   C. may constitute as mich as 25% of the total inmate population
   D. should be regarded as no different from all the other inmates

1._____

2. The passage says that today the job of handling mentally disturbed inmates is MAINLY up to

   A. psychiatric personnel   B. other inmates
   C. correction officers   D. administrative officials

2._____

3. Of the following, which is a reason given in the passage for society's failure to provide adequate treatment programs for mentally disturbed inmates?

   A. Law-abiding citizens should not have to pay for fancy treatment programs for criminals.
   B. A person who breaks the law should not expect society to give him special help.
   C. It is impossible to tell whether an inmate is mentally disturbed.
   D. There are not enough trained people to provide the kind of treatment needed.

3._____

4. The expression *abnormal individual,* as used in the last sentence of the passage, refers to an individual who is

   A. of average intelligence
   B. of superior intelligence
   C. completely normal
   D. mentally disturbed

5. The reader of the passage would MOST likely agree that

   A. correction officers should not expect mentally disturbed persons to behave the same way a normal person would behave
   B. correction officers should not report infractions of the rules committed by mentally disturbed persons
   C. mentally disturbed persons who break the law should be treated exactly the same way as anyone else
   D. mentally disturbed persons who have broken the law should not be imprisoned

Questions 6-12.

DIRECTIONS: Questions 6 through 12 are based on the roster of patients, the instructions, the table, and the sample question given below.

Twelve patients of a mental institution are divided into three permanent groups in their workshop. They must be present and accounted for in these groups at the beginning of each workday. During the day, the patients check out of their groups for various activities. They check back in again when those activities have been completed. Assume that the day is divided into three activity periods.

ROSTER OF PATIENTS

GROUP X	Ted	Frank	George	Harry
GROUP Y	Jack	Ken	Larry	Mel
GROUP Z	Phil	Bob	Sam	Vic

The following table shows the movements of these patients from their groups during the day. Assume that all were present and accounted for at the beginning of Period I.

		GROUP X	GROUP Y	GROUP Z
Period I	Check-outs	Ted, Frank	Ken, Larry	Phil
Period II	Check-ins	Frank	Ken, Larry	Phil
	Check-outs	George	Jack, Mel	Bob, Sam, Vic
Period III	Check-ins	George	Mel, Jack	Sam, Bob, Vic
	Check-outs	Frank, Harry	Ken	Vic

SAMPLE QUESTION: At the end of Period II, the patients remaining in Group X were

   A. Ted, Frank, Harry
   B. Frank, Harry
   C. Ted, George
   D. Frank, Harry, George

During Period I, Ted and Frank were checked out from Group X. During Period II, Frank was checked back in and George was checked out. Therefore, the members of the group remaining out are Ted and George. The two other members of the group, Frank and Harry, should be present. The CORRECT answer is B.

6. At the end of Period I, the TOTAL number of patients remaining in their own permanent groups was

    A. 8 B. 7 C. 6 D. 5

7. At the end of Period I, the patients remaining in Group Z were

    A. George and Harry B. Jack and Mel
    C. Bob, Sam, and Vic D. Phil

8. At the end of Period II, the patients remaining in Group Y were

    A. Ken and Larry B. Jack, Ken, and Mel
    C. Jack and Ken D. Ken, Mel, and Larry

9. At the end of Period II, the TOTAL number of patients remaining in their own permanent groups was

    A. 8 B. 7 C. 6 D. 5

10. At the end of Period II, the patients who were NOT present in Group Z were

    A. Phil, Bob, and Sam B. Sam, Bob, and Vic
    C. Sam, Vic, and Phil D. Vic, Phil, and Bob

11. At the end of Period II, the patients remaining in Group Y were

    A. Ted, Frank, and George B. Jack, Mel, and Ken
    C. Jack, Larry, and Mel D. Frank and Harry

12. At the end of Period III, the TOTAL number of patients NOT present in their own permanent groups was

    A. 4 B. 5 C. 6 D. 7

13. The one of the following conditions which bears no causative relationship to feeblemindedness is

    A. heredity B. cerebral defect
    C. early postnatal trauma D. dementia

14. Physical conditions which are caused by emotional conflicts are generally referred to as being

    A. psycho-social B. hypochondriacal
    C. psychosomatic D. psychotic

15. Of the following conditions, the one in which anxiety is NOT generally found is

    A. psychopathic personality
    B. mild hysteria
    C. psychoneurosis
    D. compulsive-obsessive personality

16. Kleptomania may BEST be described as a

    A. neurotic drive to accumulate personal property through compulsive acts in order to dispose of it to others with whom one wishes friendship
    B. type of neurosis which manifests itself in an uncontrollable impulse to steal without economic motivation
    C. psychopathic trait which is probably hereditary in nature
    D. manifestation of punishment-inviting behavior based upon guilt feelings for some other crime or wrong-doing, fantasied or real, committed as a child

17. The one of the following tests which is NOT ordinarily used as a protective technique is the

    A. Wechsler Bellevue Scale
    B. Rorschach Test
    C. Thematic Apperception Test
    D. Jung Free Association Test

18. The outstanding personality test in use at the present time is the Rorschach Test. Of the following considerations, the GREATEST value of this test to the psychiatrist and social worker is that it

    A. provides practical recommendations with reference to further educational and vocational training possibilities for the person tested
    B. reveals in quick, concise form the hereditary factors affecting the individual personality
    C. helps in substantiating a diagnosis of juvenile delinquency
    D. helps in a diagnostic formulation and in determining differential treatment

19. Of the following, the one through which ethical values are MOST generally acquired is

    A. heredity
    B. early training in school
    C. admonition and strict corrective measures by parents and other supervising adults
    D. integration into the self of parental values and attitudes

20. Delinquent behavior is MOST generally a result of

    A. living and growing up in an environment that is both socially and financially deprived
    B. a lack of educational opportunity for development of individual skills
    C. multiple factors -- psychological, bio-social, emotional and environmental
    D. low frustration tolerance of many parents toward problems of married life

21. Alcoholism in the United States is USUALLY caused by

    A. the sense of frustration in one's work
    B. inadequacy of recreational facilities
    C. neurotic conflicts expressed in drinking excessively
    D. shyness and timidity

22. The MOST distinctive characteristic of the chronic alcoholic is that he drinks alcohol 22.____

    A. socially	B. compulsively
    C. periodically	D. secretly

23. The chronic alcoholic is the person who cannot face reality without alcohol, and yet 23.____
    whose adequate adjustment to reality is impossible so long as he uses alcohol.
    On the basis of this statement, it is MOST reasonable to conclude that individuals
    overindulge in alcohol because alcohol

    A. deadens the sense of conflict, giving the individual an illusion of social competence
       and a feeling of well-being and success
    B. provides the individual with an outlet to display his feelings of good-fellowship and
       cheerfulness which are characteristic of his extroverted personality
    C. affords an escape technique from habitual irrational fears, but does not affect rational fears
    D. offers an escape from imagery and feelings of superiority which cause tension and
       anxiety

24. The one of the following drugs to which a person is LEAST likely to become addicted is 24.____

    A. opium	B. morphine	C. marijuana	D. heroin

25. Teenagers who become addicted to the use of drugs are MOST generally 25.____

    A. mentally defective	B. paranoid
    C. normally adventurous	D. emotionally disturbed

26. In the light of the current high rate of addiction to drugs among youths throughout the 26.____
    country, the one of the following statements which is generally considered to be LEAST
    correct is that

    A. a relatively large number of children and youths who experiment with drugs
       become addicts
    B. youths who use narcotics do so because of some emotional and personality disturbance
    C. youthful addicts are found largely among those who suffer to an abnormal extent
       deprivations in their personal development and growth
    D. the great majority of youthful addicts have had unfortunate home experiences and
       practically no contact with established community agencies

27. The one of the following terms which BEST describes the psychological desire to repeat 27.____
    the use of a drug intermittently or continously because of emotional needs is

    A. habituation	B. euphoria	C. tolerance	D. addiction

28. The desire for special clothing in a mental institution usually is concerned with 28.____

    A. shoes	B. sox	C. trousers	D. underwear

29. A study entitled "A preliminary evaluation of the relationship between group psychotherapy 29.____
    and the adjustment of adolescent inmates (16-21 years) in a short-term penal institution"
    was conducted by the Diagnostic Staff at Rikers Island in New York. A conclusion
    which was drawn as a result of the study was that

A. a repetition of the study was necessary with smaller therapy and non-therapy groups
B. group psychotherapy subjects displayed a better institutional adjustment than those not receiving group therapy
C. no follow-up study was necessary because of the negative results from the original study
D. a smaller proportion of experimental group subjects improved after receiving group psychotherapy when compared to those who did not receive group therapy

30. The one of the following statements which is MOST accurate concerning group psychotherapy is that group psychotherapy

   A. is in a way an outgrowth of the concept of patient self-government
   B. is of little value with deviant personality types
   C. should make the group members resent help from their fellow patients
   D. reflects a punitive rather than a rehabilitative aim

31. In group counseling and psychotherapy it is USUALLY true that persons are more defensive and argumentative than in individualized counseling and therapy sessions. The reason for this tendency is that

   A. individuals in a group setting feel it more necessary to protect their personality
   B. people in group settings are motivated by the characteristically free atmosphere
   C. people would rather argue in a group setting than in an individualized setting
   D. the group session is more poorly organized and therefore uncontrolled

32. There is a group of mentally ill patients who have a <u>functional psychosis.</u> The word "functional" in this case indicates that

   A. it is an organic psychosis
   B. the psychosis is caused by alcoholism or drug addiction
   C. there are no demonstrable changes in the brain
   D. there are clinical findings of senile arteriosclerosis

33. "Sociopaths" is a fairly new word used to describe

   A. confirmed narcotics addicts
   B. latent male homosexuals
   C. neurotic adolescents
   D. psychopathic personalities

34. The incarceration of the geriatric presents many problems in mental administration. The word "geriatric" means MOST NEARLY

   A. dipsomanic (alcoholic)
   B. moronic (mentally deficient)
   C. pertaining to split personality types
   D. pertaining to individuals of advanced years

35. Jobs for ex-patients can MOST often be found in

   A. big corporations
   B. domestic service
   C. government agencies
   D. small private enterprises

KEY (CORRECT ANSWERS)

1.	C	16.	B
2.	C	17.	A
3.	D	18.	D
4.	D	19.	D
5.	A	20.	C
6.	B	21.	C
7.	C	22.	B
8.	A	23.	A
9.	D	24.	C
10.	B	25.	D
11.	C	26.	A
12.	B	27.	A
13.	D	28.	A
14.	C	29.	B
15.	A	30.	A

31. A
32. C
33. D
34. D
35. D

EXAMINATION SECTION
TEST 1

DIRECTIONS: Each question or incomplete statement is followed by several suggested answers or completions. Select the one that BEST answers the question or completes the statement. *PRINT THE LETTER OF THE CORRECT ANSWER IN THE SPACE AT THE RIGHT.*

1. The one of the following diseases which is the LEADING cause of death in the 10-to-15 year age group is
   A. cancer B. tuberculosis C. poliomyelitis
   D. diabetes E. rheumatic fever

   1._____

2. The one of the following which would MOST likely be a result of untreated syphilis is
   A. paresis B. phlebitis C. carcinoma
   D. silicosis E. angina pectoris

   2._____

3. The one of the following which is MOST likely to be used in establishing a diagnosis of epilepsy is a(n)
   A. electrocardiogram B. spinal x-ray
   C. fluoroscopic examination D. electroencephalogram
   E. psychometric examination

   3._____

4. The pathology of diabetes involves the FAILURE of the body to produce an adequate supply of
   A. sugar B. carbohydrates C. insulin
   D. salt E. bile

   4._____

5. The one of the following statements that is TRUE about diabetes is that
   A. it can generally be cured if medical orders are followed
   B. it can generally be kept under control but not cured
   C. it is an infectious disease
   D. blindness is an inevitable result of it
   E. controlled diabetes is a progressively disabling disease

   5._____

6. Scurvy is caused by a deficiency of vitamin
   A. A B. B C. C D. E E. K

   6._____

7. Vitamin D deficiency is common because
   A. it can only be injected
   B. it is generally associated with poorly tasting foods
   C. only physicians can administer it
   D. it is not found naturally in many foods

   7._____

8. The one of the following vitamins that is used as an aid in coagulating blood is vitamin
   A. A B. B C. C D. E E. K

   8._____

9. The one of the following statements that is TRUE of Duchenne muscular dystrophy is that
   A. it is transmitted to the male children through the mother
   B. the male is the carrier of the disease
   C. the brain is primarily affected because of a lack of blood supply
   D. it is caused by a nutritional deficiency in the antepartum period
   E. only female children are susceptible to the disease

9.____

10. If a patient is repeatedly admitted to the hospital because of a series of mishaps in which he has suffered broken bones, the one of the following that is MOST likely to be true is that he is
    A. a rigid person   B. a diabetic   C. malingering
    D. accident prone   E. psychotic

10.____

11. The one of the following groups of illnesses that is known to be caused by bacteria is
    A. mental diseases   B. acute infectious diseases
    C. nutritional diseases   D. degenerative diseases
    E. cancerous tumors

11.____

12. The one of the following with which Hodgkin's Disease is COMMONLY associated is
    A. neurasthenia   B. meningitis   C. poliomyelitis
    D. cancer   E. tuberculosis

12.____

13. The one of the following diseases in which the determination of the sedimentation rate is IMPORTANT for diagnostic purposes is
    A. rheumatic heart disease   B. congenital heart disease
    C. hypertensive heart disease   D. diabetes
    E. gonorrhea

13.____

14. The one of the following disease classifications that would INCLUDE spinal meningitis is
    A. cancer or tumor   B. nutritional disease
    C. acute infectious disease   D. focal or local infection
    E. acute poisoning or intoxication

14.____

15. The one of the following diseases that may cause visual impairment and blindness is
    A. ringworm   B. osteomyelitis
    C. poliomyelitis   D. gall bladder disease
    E. diabetes

15.____

16. The one of the following that is NOT an anesthetic is
    A. cholesterol   B. nitrous oxide   C. sodium pentothal
    D. procaine   E. ethyl chloride

16.____

17. The one of the following that BEST describes the restrictions to be applied to Mr. K., a cardiac patient classified, according to the standards of the American Heart Association, as functional, Class IVD, is
    A. limited activity
    B. complete bed rest
    C. four hours rest daily
    D. prohibition of stair climbing, alcohol or tobacco
    E. convalescent status

17.____

18. Over time, geriatrics has become an increasingly important branch of medicine CHIEFLY due to
    A. greater specialization within the medical profession
    B. the discovery of penicillin and aureomycin
    C. advances in medical education
    D. increases in hospitalization
    E. the increase in the span of life

18.____

19. The one of the following which is MOST likely to be an occupational disease is
    A. cancer   B. cerebral hemorrhage
    C. septicemia   D. asthma
    E. nephritis

19.____

20. The one of the following that is a NUTRITIONAL disease is
    A. tuberculosis   B. scurvy   C. hepatitis
    D. lymphoma   E. scabies

20.____

21. Morbidity rate refers to the
    A. incidence of an illness
    B. ratio of births to deaths
    C. bacterial count
    D. degree of disability caused by an illness
    E. death rate

21.____

22. A pediatrician is a doctor who specializes in the treatment of
    A. children   B. foot diseases
    C. disabling illnesses D. orthopedic diseases
    E. the aged

22.____

23. A sadistic person is one who
    A. receives gratification through suffering pain
    B. secures a great deal of satisfaction from his own body
    C. receives gratification from inflicting pain on others
    D. turns all feelings towards others back into his own personality
    E. seeks solace through deep mental depression

23.____

24. The one of the following which is said to be the masculine counterpart of the *Electra Complex* is the _____ complex.
    A. sexual perversion   B. frustration   C. Oedipus
    D. reanimation   E. repression

24.____

25. The one of the following conditions for which a patient would be admitted to a state mental hospital is
    A. schizophrenia
    B. muscular dystrophy
    C. pathological lying
    D. congenital syphilis
    E. psychoneurosis

26. The one of the following statements which BEST describes the difference between a hallucination and a delusion is that
    A. hallucinations occur only at night
    B. delusions occur only with menopause
    C. delusions are primarily provoked by sexual function
    D. a hallucination has a basis in beliefs or ideas
    E. a delusion has a basis in beliefs or ideas

27. Finger sucking in early childhood has long been a subject of discussion among psychiatrists.
    The one of the following statements that is GENERALLY accepted as true is that
    A. finger sucking denotes pending neuroses and the parents need psychiatric consultation
    B. finger sucking is a normal activity of early childhood and should not be interfered with
    C. finger sucking alters the child's facial contours and should be heavily discouraged
    D. finger sucking by a child over nine months old is due to emotional upset and needs treatment
    E. the physician should discuss possible remedial measures such as guards on fingers

28. The one of the following who is said to be the *Father of Medicine* is
    A. Hippocrates
    B. Pasteur
    C. Galen
    D. Sydenham
    E. Plato

29. The one of the following who is credited with the improvement of conditions in mental hospitals and the founding of new ones in the United States is
    A. Andrew Jackson
    B. Dorothea Dix
    C. William Knowlton
    D. Robert Stack
    E. Rene Laennec

30. The one of the following doctors whose name is COMMONLY associated with much of the early growth and subsequent progress of medical social work is Dr.
    A. Sigmund Freud
    B. Richard C. Cabot
    C. Elizabeth Blackwell
    D. Carmyn Lombardo
    E. Thomas Parran

KEY (CORRECT ANSWERS)

1.	A	11.	B	21.	A
2.	A	12.	D	22.	A
3.	D	13.	A	23.	C
4.	C	14.	C	24.	C
5.	B	15.	E	25.	A
6.	C	16.	A	26.	E
7.	D	17.	B	27.	B
8.	E	18.	E	28.	A
9.	A	19.	D	29.	B
10.	D	20.	B	30.	B

EXAMINATION SECTION
TEST 1

DIRECTIONS: Each question or incomplete statement is followed by several suggested answers or completions. Select the one that BEST answers the question or completes the statement. *PRINT THE LETTER OF THE CORRECT ANSWER IN THE SPACE AT THE RIGHT.*

1. Which of the following statements is TRUE?

    A. The goal of normalization is to allow one to do whatever one likes.
    B. Normalization involves making a person become normal.
    C. Normalization advocates that whenever possible, people's perceptions of developmentally disabled individuals must be enhanced or improved.
    D. Normalization advocates encouraging the developmentally disabled to be just like everyone else.

2. It is important to view the developmentally disabled as

    A. helpless
    B. unable to make decisions
    C. deviant
    D. none of the above

3. All of the following would be considered good practice EXCEPT

    A. providing residential services in the community, rather than in an isolated area
    B. placing residential homes next to rural prisons
    C. providing access in residences to accommodate those who are non-ambulatory
    D. avoiding excessive rules that tend to separate staff from residents

4. All of the following are true in normalization EXCEPT

    A. family involvement in normalization is usually not helpful to achieving the goal
    B. clients should be involved, when possible, in selecting programming in order to develop independence
    C. program options should emphasize autonomy, independence, integration, and productivity
    D. it is a good idea when possible to have day programming located apart from the living setting

5. Benefits of normalization include all of the following EXCEPT

    A. development of self-confidence and self-esteem in the developmentally disabled
    B. social integration of the developmentally disabled
    C. positive changes in societal attitudes regarding the developmentally disabled
    D. societal acceptance of deviance

6. All of the following statements are true EXCEPT:

    A. Normalization means that normal conditions of life should be made available to developmentally disabled people
    B. Attitudes toward the mentally retarded have a great effect on the way they are treated, and, consequently, on their chances for living a productive, normal life

C. It is highly unlikely that efforts at normalization will succeed in most communities
D. What is normal or typical in one society may not be normal or typical in another

7. In normalization, the means used to teach a skill are as important as the skill itself. In teaching adults, which of the following would be MOST appropriate?

    A. Working individually with someone after dinner in order to teach him or her how to brush their teeth
    B. Teaching pouring skills with sand in a sandbox
    C. Teaching how to button clothes by using a doll for practice
    D. Teaching how to tie shoelaces by first working With a baby shoe

8. Which of the following statements is TRUE?

    A. Residents' chore duties in a community residence should only change three times a year.
    B. Entrance into a community residence should be solely determined by an individual's need for a place to live.
    C. Using a task analysis for a client would involve breaking down a complex task into smaller, more understandable parts.
    D. Clients should be allowed to eat when and what they choose.

9. Select the one statement below that is NOT true of supervised community residences. A supervised community residence

    A. can provide short-term residence for individuals who need only training and experience in activities of daily living after a period of institutionalization or as an alternative to institutionalization
    B. can provide an institutional setting for those people who need it
    C. can provide long-term residence for individuals who are unlikely to acquire the skills necessary for more independent living
    D. usually requires staff on site at all times

10. All of the following are goals of community residences EXCEPT

    A. providing a home environment for developmentally disabled persons
    B. providing a setting where clients can learn the skills necessary to live in the least restrictive environment
    C. providing a setting where the developmentally disabled can acquire the skills necessary to live as independently as possible
    D. the community residence allows for the maximum level of independence inconsistent with a person's disability and functional level

11. All of the following statements are true EXCEPT:

    A. A community residence does not need to adhere to the principle of normalization in its physical or social structure
    B. The term least restrictive environment refers to an environment which most resembles that of non-handicapped peers where the needs of developmentally disabled persons can be met

C. A person's length of stay in a community residence extends only until a person has attained the skills and motivation to function successfully in a less restrictive setting
D. The purposes of a community residence may vary so that people with different ranges of abilities and levels of functioning may be served

12. All of the following statements are true EXCEPT: 12.____

    A. Developmentally disabled persons residing in community residences must be afforded privacy, personal space, and freedom of access to the house as is consistent with their age and program needs
    B. Transportation should be available from the nearest institution so that people in community residences have access to the community
    C. The service needs of each person in a community residence should be individually planned by an interdisciplinary team
    D. An interdisciplinary team should include staff of the community residence, providers of program and support services, and, if appropriate, the developmentally disabled person's correspondent

13. All of the following statements are true EXCEPT: 13.____

    A. Supportive community residences are not required to provide staff on site 24 hours a day
    B. Residents in supervised community residences may need more assistance in activities of daily living than persons residing in supportive community residences
    C. An aim of a community residence is to maintain a family and home-like environment
    D. Those living in a community residence shall spend at least three hours per weekday and one evening per week in programs and activities at the residence

14. In working in treatment teams, it is MOST important for team members to 14.____

    A. communicate effectively with each other
    B. keep morale high
    C. attend meetings on time
    D. enjoy working with each other

15. All of the following statements are true EXCEPT: 15.____

    A. In teaching self-care skills, many tasks may need to be divided into sub-parts
    B. Tasks which are easiest to learn should generally be taught first
    C. Changes in routine are very helpful when teaching the mentally retarded a new skill
    D. The severely retarded do not learn as well from verbal instruction as they do from demonstration of a skill

16. All of the following statements are true EXCEPT: 16.____

    A. It is important to evaluate the client's readiness to attempt learning a particular task before starting to teach the task
    B. It is better to do a task for a client if the task may take much time and effort on his or her part
    C. People generally learn faster when their efforts lead to an enjoyable activity
    D. It is best when teaching a certain skill to begin with a small group when possible

17. All of the following statements are true EXCEPT:

    A. The expectations of a staff person of how well a client will be able to perform a certain task can influence daily living skills
    B. Environmental factors can influence daily living skills
    C. After seeing a skill demonstrated, a client should practice the skill
    D. A client will make a greater effort if he or she feels ill at ease with the instructor, and knows the instructor will become impatient if he or she continues to make mistakes

18. Of the following, the BEST way to teach a client an activity of daily living is to

    A. describe the steps to the client
    B. read the directions to the client
    C. break the activity into steps and have the client learn one step at a time
    D. have a client who can perform the task teach the client who cannot

19. All of the following are important steps in teaching a living skill EXCEPT

    A. defining the skill clearly
    B. determining the size of the skill
    C. breaking down each major step into substeps and sub-substeps as necessary
    D. rewarding the accomplishment of each step with candy

20. When teaching a daily living skill, it is important to keep in mind all of the following EXCEPT

    A. using concrete and specific language
    B. punishment can be a highly effective learning device
    C. matching the size of the skill to the client's ability level
    D. demonstrating what you want the resident to do

KEY (CORRECT ANSWERS)

1.	C	11.	A
2.	D	12.	B
3.	B	13.	D
4.	A	14.	A
5.	D	15.	C
6.	C	16.	B
7.	A	17.	D
8.	C	18.	C
9.	B	19.	D
10.	D	20.	B

TEST 2

DIRECTIONS: Each question or incomplete statement is followed by several suggested answers or completions. Select the one that BEST answers the question or completes the statement. *PRINT THE LETTER OF THE CORRECT ANSWER IN THE SPACE AT THE RIGHT.*

1. All of the following would be considered qualities of a developmental disability EXCEPT the disability   1.____

    A. may be attributable to mental retardation or autism
    B. has continued or can be expected to continue indefinitely
    C. can be easily overcome
    D. may be attributable to cerebral palsy or neurological impairment

2. The condition of autism   2.____

    A. applies to those people who have little or no control over their motor skills
    B. is hereditary
    C. is characterized by severe disorders of communication and behavior
    D. begins most frequently in adulthood

3. Secondary childhood autism differs from primary childhood autism in that   3.____

    A. primary childhood autism is more difficult to treat
    B. secondary childhood autism is secondary to disturbances such as brain damage
    C. secondary childhood autism is not as severe a disorder
    D. secondary childhood autism is less likely to interfere with behavior patterns

4. Which of the following would be LEAST adversely affected by autism?   4.____

    A. Interpersonal relations
    B. Learning
    C. Developmental rate and sequences
    D. Motor skills

5. Which of the following statements is NOT true?   5.____

    A. Cerebral palsy refers to a condition resulting from damage to the brain that may occur before, during or after birth and results in the loss of control over voluntary muscles in the body.
    B. Ataxic cerebral palsy is characterized by an inability to maintain normal balance.
    C. Someone with athetoid cerebral palsy would find it easier to maintain purposefulness of movements than someone with spastic cerebral palsy.
    D. Mixed cerebral palsy refers to the combination of two or more of the following categories of cerebral palsy such as the spastic, athetoid, ataxic, tremor, and rigid types.

6. All of the following are true about epilepsy EXCEPT   6.____

    A. epilepsy does not usually involve a loss of consciousness
    B. an *aura* often appears to the individual before a *grand mal* seizure occurs

C. people experiencing *petit mal* seizures are seldom aware that a seizure has occurred
D. status epilepticus, psychomotor, and Jacksonian are all forms of epilepsy

7. All of the following statements are true of mental retardation EXCEPT:

    A. The prevalence of mental retardation in the general total population is less than 3% of the population
    B. Approximately 89% of the mentally retarded population is mildly retarded
    C. School-age children who are mildly retarded can usually acquire practical skills and useful reading and arithmetic skills
    D. Adults who are mildly retarded can not usually achieve social and vocational skills adequate for minimum self-support

8. Which of the following statements is NOT true of mental retardation?

    A. Approximately 6% of the mentally retarded population is moderately retarded (I.Q. 36-51), 3.5% of the mentally retarded population is severely retarded (I.Q. 20-35), and 1.5% of this population is profoundly retarded (I.Q. 19 and below).
    B. A profoundly retarded person could never achieve limited self-care.
    C. Moderately retarded adults may achieve self-maintenance in unskilled work or semi-skilled work under sheltered conditions.
    D. Severely retarded children can profit from systematic skills training.

9. All of the following refer to neurological impairment EXCEPT

    A. childhood aphasia is a condition characterized by the failure to develop, or difficulty in using, language and speech
    B. epilepsy
    C. minimal brain dysfunction is associated with deviations of the central nervous system
    D. neurological impairment refers to a group of disorders of the central nervous system characterized by dysfunction in one or more, but not all, skills affecting communicative, perceptual, cognitive, memory, attentional, motor control, and appropriate social behaviors

10. Which of the following statements is TRUE?

    A. Autistic children are below average in intelligence level.
    B. All cerebral palsied persons are mentally retarded.
    C. Once an epileptic seizure has started, it cannot be stopped.
    D. Autism is due to faulty early interactional patterns between child and mother.

11. All of the following are false EXCEPT

    A. recent investigations have found that parents of autistic children have no specific common personality traits and no unusual environmental stresses
    B. cerebral palsied persons cannot understand directions
    C. it is not true that unless controlled seizures can cause further brain damage
    D. the majority of the mentally retarded are in institutions

12. In serving the needs of autistic persons, the one of the following which is usually LEAST important is the need

    A. for training in social skills
    B. for language stimulation
    C. to deal with potentially self-injurious, repetitive, and aggressive behaviors
    D. to teach skills that would improve intelligence

13. In serving the needs of persons with cerebral palsy, the one of the following which is usually LEAST important is the need

    A. to experience normal movement and sensations as much as possible
    B. to develop fundamental movement patterns which the person can regulate
    C. for experience and guidance in social settings
    D. to restrict their environment

14. All of the following statements are true EXCEPT:

    A. It is important that epileptic persons have balanced diets
    B. Pica, a craving for unnatural food, occurs with all mentally retarded persons
    C. It has been projected that 50% of those individuals who have cerebral palsy are also mentally retarded
    D. When working with the mentally retarded, it is important to encourage sensory-motor stimulation, physical stimulation, language stimulation, social skills training, and the performance of daily living skills

15. When working with neurologically impaired persons, all of the following are true EXCEPT:

    A. There is usually a need for perceptual training
    B. It is important to keep in mind that an individual may know something one day and not know it the next
    C. It may be necessary to remove distracting stimuli
    D. It is important to keep in mind that neurologically impaired persons usually have substantially lower I.Q.'s than the average person

16. The developmentally disabled do NOT have the right to

    A. register and vote in elections
    B. marry
    C. confidentiality of records
    D. hit someone who teases them

17. Which of the following statements is TRUE?

    A. It is important for staff members not to make all of the choices for their mentally retarded clients.
    B. Distraction is not a good technique to use when trying to channel potentially violent or destructive behavior to a socially acceptable outlet.
    C. Severely and profoundly retarded children do not appear to have a strong need for personal contact.
    D. It is primarily the mildly or moderately retarded child that exhibits the behavior usually associated with mental retardation.

18. All of the following are causes of mental retardation EXCEPT

    A. organic defects
    B. brain lesions
    C. increased sexual activity
    D. chromosomal abnormalities

18._____

19. A mentally retarded patient who is *acting out*

    A. may be trying to communicate that he or she is physically uncomfortable or needs something
    B. should be ignored
    C. should be severely punished
    D. feels comfortable in his or her surroundings

19._____

20. In working with the developmentally disabled, all of the following would be appropriate EXCEPT

    A. remembering that seemingly small things, both positive and negative, can be very important to the client
    B. allowing choices whenever possible
    C. maintaining a calm, level-headed attitude during an anxiety-producing situation will reassure clients and help them relax and feel safer
    D. after basic self-help skills have been mastered, it is not necessary to encourage further development

20._____

KEY (CORRECT ANSWERS)

1.	C	11.	A
2.	C	12.	D
3.	B	13.	D
4.	D	14.	B
5.	C	15.	D
6.	A	16.	D
7.	D	17.	A
8.	B	18.	C
9.	B	19.	A
10.	C	20.	D

MANAGEMENT OF THE EMOTIONALLY DISTURBED

Unit 1. Emotional Aspects of Illness and Injury	1
Responses of Patients to Illness and Injury	1
Responses of the Family, Friends, or Bystanders	2
Responses of the Paramedic	2
Responses of Patients and Bystanders to Mass Casualties	3
Death and Dying	4
Unit 2. Psychiatric Emergencies	5
Patient Assessment and General Principles of Management	5
Specific Psychiatric Emergencies	8
Unit 3. Techniques of Management: Patient Interviewing	13

MANAGEMENT OF THE EMOTIONALLY DISTURBED

Unit 1. Emotional Aspects of Illness and Injury

Everyone involved in a critical illness or injury situation--the patient, the family, bystanders, health professionals--responds to stresses that naturally occur in such emergencies. Emergency Medical Technicians-Paramedics (EMT-P's) can deal effectively with these responses, both in others and in themselves, only if they can understand and anticipate such responses.

Responses of Patients to Illness and Injury

Although patients' reactions to critical illness or injury are largely determined by mechanisms they already have developed to deal with stressful situations, most of these reactions will follow common patterns. Patients usually become aware of painful or unpleasant sensations, and sometimes decreased energy and strength, with the onset of illness. The coon response to this awareness is anxiety. Some patients will attempt to deny or minimize their symptoms at this point, while others will become irritable and angry. The paramedic must be aware that once patients begin to see themselves as ill or to realize they have been injured, the following reactions may occur:

- Realistic fears. Patients may fear pain, disability, death, or financial problems. Such fears are normal and reasonable in ill or injured patients.
- General anxiety. Feelings of loss of control are common among ill or injured patients. They may feel helpless knowing they are completely dependent on someone else, often a stranger, whose knowledge of medical care and ability they cannot evaluate easily. Patients whose self-esteem depends on being active, independent, and aggressive are particularly prone to anxiety in these situations.
- Depression. Depression is a natural response by some patients to the loss of some bodily function as well as to feelings of loss of control over his or her own destiny.
- Regression. Patients may return to earlier or more primitive modes of behavior. Their behavior may appear childlike. This is natural as ill or injured patients, like children, must depend on others for their survival.
- Denial. Many patients try to deny or ignore the seriousness of their illness or injury because it causes them anxiety. Denial often is seen as a tendency to dismiss all symptoms with words like "only" or "a little." When a patient uses this mechanism, the paramedic may need to find an informant among the patient's family or friends from whom a more accurate history can be obtained.
- Displacement of anger. Patients often respond to discomfort or limitations of activity by becoming resentful and suspicious of those around them. They may vent this anger on the paramedic by becoming impatient and irritable or excessively demanding. It is important for the paramedic to realize that the patient's anger stems from fear and discomfort and is not really directed at the paramedic.
- Confusion. Illness or injury can cause disorientation among patients, especially the elderly. Such confusion is increased by the presence of unfamiliar people and equipment. In these cases, it is important for paramedics to explain carefully who they are and what they plan to do and to explain treatment steps as they are being performed.

In addition, patients usually will have uncomfortable feelings about being examined. Ordinarily, undressing in front of another person is done in situations of intimacy and trust. Thus, every patient will feel some anxiety about having a stranger perform a physical examination. Some patients may consider the physical exam a humiliating invasion of privacy. Therefore, the paramedic always should try to establish a relationship with the patient during an initial interview and then conduct the physical examination. Furthermore, the paramedic always should be aware of the unclothed patient's probable embarrassment and shame and make sure that the patient is properly draped or shielded from the stares of curious bystanders. The EMT-P should conduct the examination in an efficient, businesslike manner and continue talking with the patient during the entire procedure.

Responses of the Family Friends or Bystanders

Those at the scene with the patient also may show many of the responses described above. Family members may be anxious, panicky, or angry. Their anger often results from their feelings of guilt. As a means of coping with their own anxiety, they may demand immediate action, or they may pressure the paramedic to move the patient to the hospital before appropriate examination and stabilization have been completed. They may state or imply that the paramedic is not competent to handle the situation ("Get him to the hospital so he can be seen by a doctor."). No matter how upsetting this may be, a paramedic must realize that the patient's family and friends are concerned and that their behavior, however irritating to the paramedic, arises from distress. The paramedic should remain calm and sympathetic and explain treatment activities to friends and family members. They should be reassured that paramedics are in radio contact with physicians at all times and are acting under a physician's direction to help the patient.

Responses of the Paramedic

Health professionals are not immune to the stresses of emergency situations. When dealing with the critically ill and injured, they may experience a wide range of feelings, some of which are unpleasant. The paramedic may feel irritated by the family or the patient's demands, be anxious when faced with life-threatening injuries, become defensive at implications that he or she is not competent to handle emergencies, and become sad in response to tragedy. Although these feelings are natural, it is best for the paramedic not to express them during an emergency. Furthermore, if the EMT-P gives an outward appearance of calmness and confidence, it will help to relieve the anxiety of those on the scene. Helping others to remain calm is part of the paramedic's therapeutic role.

Another common reaction among health professionals is irritation with the patient who does not appear particularly ill. This reaction can be a special problem of emergency personnel, who are prepared to deal with life-threatening problems and may regard minor complaints as burdensome and annoying. It should be remembered, however, that people call for help only if they are worried about something. Patients may be worried about injuries, pains, disturbing feelings, or bodily functions that they think are abnormal. It is not the duty of the EMT-P to judge whether such complaints are real or imagined. These complaints are always real to the patient. Although it is more dramatic to rescue the multiple trauma victim than to reassure the patient with a minor cold, both patients have indicated that they are distressed and want help. In both cases, the EMT-P must be supportive and nonjudgmental and render whatever care is needed.

Responses of Patients and Bystanders to Mass Casualties

When there are multiple casualties--as in an automobile accident with several victims or a natural disaster (tornado, flood, earthquake)--both victims and bystanders may become dazed, disorganized, or overwhelmed. The American Psychiatric Association has identified five possible types of reactions in such situations:

- Normal reaction. In multiple casualty situations, the normal reaction consists of symptoms of extreme anxiety, including sweating, shaking, weakness, nausea, and sometimes vomiting. Individuals experiencing this type of response may recover completely within a few minutes and can be helpful if given clear instructions.
- Blind panic. In this type of reaction, the individual's judgment seems to disappear completely. Blind panic is particularly dangerous because it may lead to mass panic among others present.
- Depression. The individual who remains motionless and looks numbed or dazed is depressed. It is important to give such a person a task to perform in order to bring him or her back to reality.
- Overreaction. The person who talks compulsively, jokes inappropriately, and races from one task to another, usually accomplishing little, is overreacting to a situation.
- Conversion hysteria. The person's mood may shift rapidly from extreme anxiety to relative calmness. The person may convert anxiety to some bodily dysfunction. This reaction can result in hysterical blindness, deafness, or paralysis.

Paramedics should observe the following guidelines in dealing with mass casualty situations:

- Identify themselves and take command of the situation. Strive to remain self-assured and sympathetic, and conduct themselves in a businesslike manner.
- Treat serious physical injuries immediately, and reassure anxious patients or bystanders.
- Keep spectators away from the patients, but do not leave the patients alone. If all rescue personnel are busy dealing with physical injuries, assign a responsible bystander to stay with any person showing unusual behavioral symptoms.
- Assign tasks to bystanders to keep them occupied. Feeling that they are useful and responsible will lessen their anxiety greatly.
- Respect the right of patients to have their own feelings. Let the patients know that the paramedics are trying to understand their feelings so they can help. Paramedics should not try to tell the patients how they should feel.
- Accept patients' physical and emotional limitations. Fear and panic are as disabling as physical injuries, and some people are able to deal with anxiety better than others. Do not try to force patients to deal with more than they seem able to cope with. Help patients to recognize and use their remaining strength and lessen their anxiety.
- Employ sedatives only as a last resort. In most cases, they only add to the patient's confusion. In the physically injured, they may mask important symptoms. The calm, reassuring attitude of the paramedic is better, more effective therapy.
- Accept personal limitations. In mass casualty situations realize that there are limits to what can be done. Avoid overextending themselves and provide more effective care by establishing care priorities.

Death and Dying

The paramedics' contacts with the dying usually will be confined to the seriously ill or injured patient who is slipping in and out of consciousness. Occasionally, however, paramedics will encounter dying patients who are conscious and aware of their condition. Although everything possible should be done to attend to the patients' physical needs, paramedics should not neglect the emotional and religious needs of dying patients. In such situations, paramedics can reduce the apprehension of the dying to some degree by being as reassuring as-possible. Patients can be told that every effort is being made to transport them quickly to the hospital where expert help is available.

Many patients will be anxious about their family members and may express the desire to communicate with them. Paramedics may be able to reduce the anxiety of these patients by offering to make themselves available to the family and to convey any important messages to them. Such communications, since they may have later legal implications, should be noted carefully. Survivors at the scene who are aware of the dying patient's condition should be reassured that everything will be done to save the patient at the scene and at the hospital.

Paramedics must be aware of and master their own feelings concerning death. Contact with dead and dying patients causes anxiety in all health professionals. If paramedics are aware that such normal reactions affect everyone, there will be less chance that their- own feelings about death will interfere with proper treatment of dying patients.

Unit 2. Psychiatric Emergencies

Psychiatric emergencies are situations in which patients display disorders of mood, thought, or behavior that are dangerous or disturbing to themselves or others. Almost all disturbed behavior represents the individual's effort to cope with internal or external stress (anxiety). Such behavior often disappears when normal psychological defense mechanisms are mobilized properly.

Most psychiatric emergencies are emergencies because the patients' disturbed behavior makes them, their families, or bystanders feel anxious or panicky. Patients and others will feel they are in a situation that is out of their control and may demand that paramedics take control by pressuring them to "do something" immediately. It is important to remember that the general excitement in such situations results from feelings of fear and loss of control. These feelings can be lessened when the EMT-P maintains a calm, self-assured attitude.

It is important to recall that <u>abnormal behavior may be due to conditions other than mental illness.</u> Diabetes, seizure disorders, severe infections, metabolic disorders, head injury, hypertension, stroke, alcohol, and other drugs all may cause disturbed behavior. Disturbed behavior is caused by intoxication with alcohol or another drug in more than half of the patients who demonstrate such behavior. These other possible causes should be remembered whenever a patient with apparent emotional disturbance is evaluated.

Primary emotional disorders are a response to personal crisis. When individuals' basic needs are threatened, they face crises that vary in severity depending on their ability to deal with their feelings. People in crisis have two alternatives: They can cope with the situation by finding ways to alter it, or they can attempt to decrease the discomfort by escaping from the situation. Escape takes many forms, including the use of alcohol or other drugs, suicide, or the manifestation of psychiatric symptoms. Such symptoms are a compromise for the patient and reduce the anxiety produced by the inner crisis.

Patient Assessment and General Principles of Management

The patient exhibiting bizarre or unusual behavior usually is in the midst of an emotional crisis. Such a patient may need immediate attention to lessen emotional distress. While attempting to alleviate the patient's anxiety, the paramedic also must prevent injury to the patient or others at the scene and attempt to bring a measure of calm to a stressful situation.

The in-depth counseling necessary to deal with a severe psychiatric reaction may not be feasible in field situations. In some cases, a crisis worker, contacted through appropriate local resources, may be more capable of managing the crisis than is the paramedic. Ideally, if the dispatcher anticipates an emotional problem, the appropriate crisis intervention team can be contacted prior to the arrival of the Emergency Medical Services (EMS) team at the scene. However, if the EMS team arrives at the scene without prior warning, paramedics must be prepared to deal with the situation within the limits of their training in crisis counseling and as best as can be expected in a field situation.

Once the paramedics arrive at the scene, they should notify the dispatcher of the presenting conditions and notify support services, such as crisis intervention teams.

Patient assessment and principles of management are presented together because the two are inseparable in dealing with emotional problems. The process of communicating with the patient through which paramedics obtain a history is therapeutic. Therefore, the approach to the disturbed patient and some specific parts of patient assessment will be discussed.

The following general guidelines are recommended to help EMT-P's with emotionally disturbed patients. Paramedics must:

- Be prepared to spend time with disturbed patients and not hurry. A lengthy discussion may be required if it provides the patients with emotional relief. Such individuals require patient, concerned attention.
- Be calm and direct. Disturbed patients often are frightened of losing self-control. Remain calm and undisturbed, thus indicating to the patients that the paramedics are confident that the patients can stay in control. Indeed, one major purpose of the interview is to help a patient regain control. Showing anxiety or panic serves only to increase a patient's belief that the situation is overwhelming.
- Clearly identify themselves. Tell the patients who the EMT crew is and what it is trying to do for them.
- Assess the patients at home or wherever the emergency occurs. Do not rush off to the hospital, which is strange and intimidating for a patient. Hurrying to the hospital also can reinforce the belief that something is terribly wrong. Let patients recover their bearings in familiar surroundings.
- Interview the patients alone, if possible. Ask relatives or bystanders to go into another room, where another EMT-P can obtain their stories.
- Sit down to interview patients. Never tower over them.
- Let the patients tell what happened in their own way. Do not attempt to direct the conversation, but allow the patients to air their feelings.
- Be interested in the patients' stories but not overly sympathetic. If a paramedic overwhelms a patient with pity, the paramedic will convince the patient that the situation is indeed hopeless. Treat a patient as someone expected to get better.
- Maintain a nonjudgmental attitude. Accept the patients' right to have their own feelings, and do not blame or criticize them for feeling as they do.
- Provide honest reassurance. Let the patients know what is expected from them and what they can expect of a paramedic.
- Present a definite plan of action. This makes patients feel that the paramedics are doing something to help and relieves their anxiety. People in crisis need direction. Do not confront patients with questions ("Do you want to go to the hospital?") but rather with statements ("I think it is important for you to go to the hospital. There are doctors there who can help you.").
- Encourage purposeful movement, as this often helps relieve anxiety. If patients will be going to the hospital, encourage them to gather up the belongings they want to bring with them. Letting patients do as much as possible for themselves can reinforce their feelings that the paramedics expect them to get better.
- Stay with the patient at all times. Raving responded to the emergency, the paramedics are responsible for the patients' safety.
- Never assume they cannot talk with any patient until they try.

The assessment should begin as soon as the EMT-P begins talking with the patient. The patient's general appearance and clothing should be noted, and it should be observed whether the patient appears neat or disheveled. The patient's rate of speech also should be noted. If it is slowed, it may suggest depression or some kind of intoxication. If it is rapid and pressured, it may suggest mania or the presence of amphetamines. The following questions should be kept in mind when assessing these patients:

- Is the patient easily distracted?
- Are the patient's responses appropriate?
- Is the patient alert and able to communicate coherently?
- Is the patient's memory intact?
- What is the patient's mood?
- Does the patient seem abnormally depressed, elated, or agitated?
- Does the patient appear fearful or worried?
- Does the patient show evidence of disordered thought, such as disturbances in judgment, delusions (false ideas), or hallucinations (seeing or hearing things that are not there)?

Initial questions should be direct and specific to establish whether the patient is alert, oriented, and able to communicate. Only information that is crucial to immediate management should be collected. Paramedics should ask the patient's full name, age, and marital status; find out what kind of work the patient does and where and with whom the patient lives; and inquire about past medical and psychiatric problems. After this, questions should be open ended, beginning with words like "What," "How," or "When." Try not to begin questions with the word "Why." ("Why did you lock everyone out of your room?"). Patients may think they are being criticized by such questions. Let them tell their stories in their own ways.

After talking with patients and gaining their confidence, paramedics should gauge the patient's ability to tolerate a physical examination. If at all possible, they should take vital signs and perform a quick neurological examination, although this may not be possible with violent or extremely fearful patients. Paramedics should do as much as they can without increasing the patient's distress. Conversation should be continued throughout the physical examination.

In general, seriously disturbed patients should be seen by a physician who can decide whether they need to be hospitalized. In most areas, there are four ways to admit patients for psychiatric care. There is "voluntary admission," in which patients sign themselves into the hospital and can leave whenever they want to. Another kind of admission is "voluntary commitment," in which patients agree to be admitted to the hospital but cannot leave until their commitment period ends. Voluntary commitments usually last 10 to 30 days, unless the patients extend the commitment.

Patients who will not agree to come to the hospital usually can be involuntarily detained and brought to the hospital by the police or family members. During this "emergency detention," the patient is examined by a psychiatrist. If the psychiatrist feels that the patient will be dangerous, he or she can authorize hospitalization for a short time, usually about 10 days. In some areas, the psychiatrist must provide evidence to the county mental health authorities to show that the patient needs to be admitted to the hospital and must obtain their permission for an emergency detention.

Many states have a procedure *known as* "court commitment," in which psychiatrists must give evidence in court that patients are mentally ill and need treatment. Some States also require that patients be considered dangerous to themselves or others before they can be committed against their will.

Involuntary commitment deprives people of their civil liberties; and, for this reason, it should not be undertaken lightly. It is not always easy, even for an experienced psychiatrist, to determine whether patients' behaviors justify removing them from society and whether they are dangerous to themselves or others. Laws on involuntary detainment vary considerably from State to State, so paramedics should become familiar with the laws in their communities. In general, patients who are conscious and alert can be taken to the hospital only with their consent. If they do not consent, patients can be taken against their will only at the request of the police. The same applies to forceful restraint. When these measures are necessary, law enforcement officers must be called. Each ambulance service should have clearly defined protocols for dealing with patients who require involuntary commitment.

Specific Psychiatric Emergencies

Psychiatric emergency situations that the paramedic is likely to encounter include those caused by depression, suicide, violent behavior, paranoia, anxiety and phobias, disorganization and disorientation, and alcohol or other drugs.

Depression. Depression can lead to a psychiatric emergency such as suicide and may cause other psychological disorders. Depressed patients may be recognized by their sad appearance, crying spells, and listless or apathetic behavior. These patients feel worthless, guilty, and extremely pessimistic. They often express the desire to be left alone, asserting that no one understands or cares about them and that their problems cannot be solved. Their speech may be halting and retarded, as if they hardly have enough energy to talk. If these patients are able to give a history, they may report that they wake at 3 or 4 a.m. and cannot get back to sleep. They also may note that they feel worse in the morning but improve during the day. Some depressed patients, however, do not feel like talking. In such cases, it may help for paramedics to confront the patients with their own observations. A comment, such as "You look very sad," often encourages patients to talk about their depressed feelings. Such patients may burst into tears and should be permitted to "cry themselves out." Patients should not be encouraged to stop crying; paramedics simply can maintain a sympathetic silence.

Every depressed patient should be questioned directly about suicidal thoughts. The paramedic might ask, for example, "Have you ever wished you were dead or thought about killing yourself?" If the response is yes, the paramedic should ask the patient how he or she would do this and determine whether the patient has made any concrete plans for suicide. Evaluating the seriousness of suicidal intentions in this way can help the paramedic decide whether the patient needs to be hospitalized.

Depressed patients need sympathetic attention and reassurance. They need to know that the paramedic is concerned about them. It usually is best if a single member of the rescue team interviews these patients in private, as the presence of several people may make depressed patients uncomfortable. Patients should be told that many people have periods of unhappiness but that they can be helped to feel better. At this point, the paramedic can mention community sources where such help can be found.

Suicide. Suicide is defined as any willful act designed to end one's own life. Suicide is most common in men, especially those who are single, widowed, or divorced. Suicide also occurs more frequently in depressed persons and alcoholics. At least 60 percent of all suicide victims attempted suicide previously, and 75 percent clearly warned that they intended to commit suicide.

Suicide attempts typically occur when close emotional attachments are in danger or when the individual loses a significant family member or friend. Suicidal people, in addition, often feel unable to manage their lives. Frequently, they lack self-esteem.

<u>Every suicidal act or gesture should be taken seriously, and the patient should be evaluated by a psychiatrist.</u>

Many people will make last minute attempts to communicate their suicidal intentions. When an individual phones to threaten suicide, someone should stay on the line with that person until the rescue squad reaches the scene. When the EMS team arrives, the area should be surveyed quickly for instruments that the individual might use to injure himself or herself; the paramedic should remove them discreetly. The EMT-P's should talk quietly with patients and encourage them to discuss their situation. Paramedics should not be afraid to ask the patients directly about suicidal thoughts. The EMT-P's should find out the following information from these patients: Have they ever attempted suicide before? Have they made any concrete plans as to how they would kill themselves? Has anyone in their families ever committed suicide? Patients who have made previous attempts, who have detailed suicide plans, or whose close relatives have attempted suicide are more likely to attempt suicide. These patients must be reassured and brought to the hospital. These patients must not be left alone under any circumstances.

When patients attempt suicide, their <u>medical</u> treatment has priority. Drug overdoses must be managed for possible respiratory depression or circulatory collapse. Patients with slashed wrists must have their bleeding controlled. Nevertheless, if patients are conscious, the EMT-P should try to talk with them and encourage them to speak about their situation. In drug overdoses, the paramedic should collect any medication containers, pills, or other drugs found near the patients and bring these with the patients to the emergency department.

<u>Rage, hostility, and violent behavior.</u> The angry, violent patient is ready to fight with anyone who approaches and may be difficult to control. It *should* be remembered that anger can be a response to illness and that aggressive behavior may be the patient's way of coping with feelings of helplessness. Paramedics should avoid responding with anger and defensiveness to the patient's behavior. If a possibility of danger exists, the patient should be interviewed with another member of the EMT crew present. Violent patients should be told briefly and honestly what they can expect from the paramedic and what the paramedic expects from them. Many angry or violent patients can be calmed by a trained person who appears confident that the patient will behave well. It also is useful to ask such patients directly about the cause of their anger with a statement such as, "I'm not sure I understand why you are angry." The patients should be reassured that the EMT-P is there to help them and is not going to punish them for their violence or anger. Such patients should be told also that talking to a doctor may help them to feel better.

A more difficult situation arises when a patient is violent and out of control. Paramedics cannot take patients to the hospital against their will. Even if this were possible, two or three paramedics might not be enough to subdue such a patient. If no one is able to communicate with these patients and it seems that they are or will be dangerous to themselves or others, paramedics must notify the police. The ENT crew can transport patients only at their own request, or when authorized by the police.

If police have authorized the transport of a violent patient to the hospital against his or her will, paramedics may need to use restraints. Restraints also require police authorization. Restraints should be padded so that they will not injure patients if they struggle against them. When paramedics apply restraints, they always should explain what they are doing, even if the patients do not appear to be listening. The patients can be told that the restraints are to protect them and others from injury. To restrain a violent patient, the paramedic should:

- Place the patient in a supine position (assuming there are no injuries).

- Apply one cravat to each wrist and ankle with a clove hitch.
- Tie the wrists and ankles together with two or more cravats.
- Secure the tails of the extremity cravats to opposite sides of the stretcher frame.
- Secure the body with two or three straps placed around the chest, waist, or upper legs. Make sure none of the straps are unduly tight or will constrict the patient's breathing.

Once restraints are applied, they must not be removed en route. Paramedics must not bargain with patients and agree to remove restraints if they promise to behave well.

If potentially violent patients are transported without restraints, the EMT-P's should make sure that patients lie down and must watch them at all times. The paramedics should position themselves between patients and the door in case a rapid exit is necessary. They should restrain patients en route if they become dangerous to themselves or others.

If a patient is suspected of being potentially homicidal, paramedics should not attempt restraint. In such situations, the paramedics' responsibilities only should involve contacting the police and removing bystanders from the scene.

<u>Paranoia.</u> Paranoid patients are suspicious and distrustful. They often are hostile and uncooperative and usually have delusions that people are out to get them. They tend to brood over real or imagined injustices, carry grudges, and recall wrongs experienced years before. Many paranoid patients also are excitable and unpredictable and have outbursts of bizarre or aggressive behavior. Their personalities often make others dislike them or feel angry with them.

When dealing with paranoid patients, paramedics must identify themselves clearly and explain what they are trying to do. The person who is paranoid may be suspicious of warmth and reassurance, so the EMT-P should maintain a friendly, but somewhat distant, neutrality. Paramedics should:

- Avoid becoming angry at the patient's anger
- Behave in a consistent manner
- Agree or disagree with the paranoid patient's statements honestly
- Use tact and firmness to persuade the patient to come to the hospital
- Gain the confidence of the patient by showing authority, self-assurance, and a genuine desire to help the individual

Paramedics should not:

- Go along with the delusions of such patients in order to pacify them.
- Interview family or friends in the patient's presence. Taking a relative aside and speaking in hushed tones only reinforces the paranoid patient's delusion that people are plotting against him or her.

<u>Anxiety and phobias.</u> Patients having anxiety attacks show evidence of intense fear. They are tense and restless and often pace and wring their hands. Tremors, tachycardia, dyspnea, sweating, and diarrhea also frequently occur. These patients feel overwhelmed and cannot concentrate. Sometimes they will hyperventilate and develop all the symptoms of that syndrome, including dizziness, tingling around the mouth and fingers, and carpopedal spasms (spasms of the hands and feet). Furthermore, the behavior of these patients creates anxiety in

those around them; therefore, they may be surrounded by a horde of anxious and excited people when the EMT crew arrives.

The first step in managing such patients is to separate them from the excited people around them. Paramedics should identify themselves and tell these patients clearly and confidently that effective treatment is available for their problems. They should be firm but supportive. They should explain what they are doing and not leave the patients alone. En route to the hospital, the paramedics should continue to reassure such patients.

Patients with phobias focus all their anxieties on one situation in the form of intense fears. Examples of phobic reactions include intense fears of high places, enclosed places, animals, weapons, and public gatherings. When these patients confront the feared situation, their anxiety becomes unbearable. When dealing with phobic patients, the paramedic must explain carefully each step involved in transporting patients to the hospital and go through each step in detail beforehand ("Then we will walk down the stairs, and I will hold your arm; then we will get into the back of the ambulance. You will sit on a bench in the ambulance, and I will be beside you."). Then the EMT-P should repeat the descriptions as the actions occur ("Now we are going down the stairs."). Such explanations will help to lessen these patients' fears.

Disorganization and disorientation. Disorganized patients are characterized by uncontrolled, disconnected thoughts. Their speech is usually incoherent or rambling, but they may be oriented to person and place. Often, such patients are found wandering aimlessly down the middle of a street, dressed peculiarly, and uttering meaningless words and sentences. Such patients need structure. The paramedic should explain what will be done and exactly 'what the patient will be expected to do. Simple, consistent, firm directions should be given. It may be impossible to get a detailed history, but the EMT-P should try to obtain the patient's name and address. These patients can be told that they need to see a doctor and that the EMT crew is planning to take them to a hospital where they can be helped.

Disoriented patients do not know where they are or what day it is and may not even know their names. This disturbance is more common among the elderly who may lapse back into memories and behave as though they were still living during an earlier period. Disorientation also can result from physical problems, including head injury, alcohol or other drug ingestion, and metabolic disorders such as diabetes. The paramedics must try to keep disoriented patients aware of the time, place, person, and situation. Patients should be told who the paramedics are and what they are doing. This may have to be repeated several times en route. The paramedics should reassure patients by such actions as pointing out landmarks that will help to orient them during the trip to the hospital.

Psychiatric emergencies caused by alcohol and other drugs

As mentioned previously, alcohol and other drugs often cause disturbed behavior. In this section, psychiatric emergencies caused by alcohol and drug use will be discussed.

Acute alcohol intoxication occurs when individuals consume enough alcohol to raise their serum alcohol levels above 150 milligrams per 100 milliliters. Signs of alcohol intoxication include poor impulse control, drowsiness, lack of coordination, slurred speech, and sometimes combativeness. If individuals are not combative, they simply should be allowed to sleep until the alcohol wears off. If they are combative, the physician may order chlorpromazine or paraldehyde to sedate them. Paramedics must remember, however, that the person who appears intoxicated may be suffering from the effects of a more serious medical problem. Therefore, these patients should be checked carefully for signs of illness or injury.

Narcotic withdrawal occurs when individuals stop taking substances to which they are physically addicted. They may develop symptoms, including restlessness, tossing sleep, yawning, watery eyes and nose, sweating, dilated pupils, goose pimples, nausea, and vomiting. Narcotic withdrawal usually is not dangerous in otherwise healthy individuals. Patients should be transported to the hospital, where withdrawal symptoms can be suppressed with narcotics and patients can be withdrawn slowly from addicting drugs. Usually the paramedic should not attempt to suppress narcotic withdrawal symptoms with morphine or meperidine in the field unless so ordered by the physician who feels that the patient may have an underlying disease that may make narcotic withdrawal dangerous. Giving narcotics to addicts in the field also can suggest to other addicts that they can obtain narcotics from the paramedic.

Barbiturate and sedative drug withdrawal symptoms resemble those of alcohol withdrawal. <u>Barbiturate withdrawal can be fatal.</u> Therefore, the physician may order the paramedic to give intravenous diazepam or phenobarbital to suppress symptoms until the patient feels drowsy. The total initial dose must be recorded accurately, since later sedative dosages given during slow withdrawal in the hospital will be determined from the initial dose. Seizures that can occur during barbiturate withdrawal can cause death. If seizures occur, they should be treated in the same manner as seizures from other causes.

Withdrawal symptoms also can occur when patients stop taking commonly prescribed sedative drugs like meprobamate, chiordiazepoxide, and diazepam. These drugs can cause withdrawal symptoms, including insomnia, anxiety, loss of appetite, vomiting, tremors, muscle twitching,, and seizures. Seizures from sedative withdrawal are treated in the same way as seizures from other causes.

The paramedic's manner and attitude during the initial contact with the patient are the most important factors in determining later events. By striving to maintain an attitude of calmness, self-confidence, sympathy, and firmness, the EMT-P often can make the difference between success and failure in handling a psychiatric emergency.

Unit 3. Techniques of Management Patient Interviewing

After the paramedic obtains basic identifying information about the patient (name, age, address), a limited interview can be conducted even in field situations. The situation will dictate the scope of the interview. Only information critical to field management should be collected, unless volunteered by the patient. The interview should be open-ended; that is, patients should not be directed but rather should be allowed to tell their stories in their own way.

To make the interview easier, the paramedic should:

- Begin the interview with an open-ended question ("What problems have you been having?").
- Give patients the floor. Do not be afraid of silences, even though they may. seem intolerably long sometimes. Maintain an attentive, relaxed attitude. It is especially important to be silent when patients stop speaking because they are overwhelmed by emotion. Avoid the temptation to soothe patients and to prevent such expressions of emotion as crying. Expressions of emotion often are therapeutic, and patients usually will express themselves more easily after their intense emotions are released. Silence also allows the patients to gain control of themselves in their own way.
- Encourage patients to communicate by making gestures such as nodding the head or using noncommittal words or phrases ("Go on" or "I see"). This technique, called facilitation, also can be used to return patients to topics for which more information is needed. For example, a patient may have referred briefly to suicidal thoughts and then moved on to another subject. When he or she finishes with the new subject, the paramedic might say, "You say you have thought of suicide?" This suggests to the patient that the paramedic is interested in what the patient has said and would like to learn more.
- Point out to the patients something of interest in their conversation or behavior of which they may not be aware. This technique, known as confrontation, describes how patients appear to the interviewer, based on the interviewer's observations, not judgments. For example, the interviewer might remark, "You seem worried," or "You sound very angry." Such comments often lead to freer expressions of feelings. They must be made, however, in a way that is neither critical nor condescending.
- o If necessary, ask questions to keep the interview moving,but make them as nondirective as possible. Avoid questions that can be answered with a simple yes or no. "How" and "what" questions are better.
- Provide support and reassurance through actions that demonstrate interest in the patient throughout the entire interview. Reassurance should never be unrealistic or foster unreasonable expectations ("You have nothing at all to worry about.") Instead, identify the patient's strengths and reinforce them ("Despite all the troubles you have had, you seem to have done a very good job at work.").

It should be noted that some patients find it difficult to deal with the lack of structure in nondirective questioning. This is true particularly of adolescents, severely depressed patients, and confused or disorganized patients. In such cases, when open-ended questions are met with uncomprehending silence, a more structured interview may produce better results.

MENTAL DISORDERS AND TREATMENT PRACTICES

This section reviews eight areas that are usually tested on examinations:

- The Characteristics of Various Psychiatric Disorders
- The Needs of Special Groups (Children, Geriatrics)
- The Influences of Environment, Society, and Family on Psychiatric Disorders
- Psychotropic Drugs (Reactions and Uses)
- The Assessment and Evaluation of Patients
- The Functions and Purposes of the Treatment Team
- The Development and Implementation of the Treatment Plan
- Methods for Handling People with Various Emotional or Psychiatric Disorders

THE CHARACTERISTICS OF VARIOUS PSYCHIATRIC DISORDERS

It is often difficult to assign labels to human behavior with any large degree of accuracy. Behavior sometimes changes rapidly, and the interpretation of what behavior a label actually represents can vary greatly from one person to the next. One can often learn a great deal more about a person by observing their behavior than by reading a diagnostic label about that person. Regardless, diagnostic labels can be helpful to members of a treatment team as a shorthand method of describing a group of behaviors one might expect from certain individuals. They are also required for many insurance forms. A diagnosis may be useful as long as one views the diagnosis as an ongoing process, and can continue to look at the patient with *new eyes*.

The Difference Between Neurosis and Psychosis

People suffering from a neurosis are usually able to manage with the concerns of daily life, although there is often some distortion in their concept of reality. Those suffering from a neurosis may feel inferior, unloved, or have a long-term feeling of fear or dread. They may have obsessions, compulsions or phobias, but they are rarely dangerous to themselves or others. They usually have some insight into their problems, and except in severe cases, don't require hospitalization. Many go through life without obtaining any help for their problems. Those who experience a psychosis, however, are out of touch with reality and live in an imaginary world. They may hear voices, feel that they are being persecuted, or experience very deep depressions. There is a very definite split between the reality of those suffering from psychoses and the reality of the world. Unlike those suffering from neuroses, those suffering from psychoses often lose track of time, person, and place, and they have little insight into the nature of their behavior. They usually require hospitalization and their behavior is sometimes injurious to other people or themselves, although they may insist that there is nothing wrong with them.

Categories of Neurosis

It is important to keep in mind that rarely will all of a patient's symptoms fall into any one category, and that symptoms may change over time from one category to another. *Anxiety Neuroses* constitute approximately 35% of all neurotic disorders. Those suffering from anxiety neuroses have a tendency to view the world as hostile and cruel, and may frequently restrict daily activities in order to feel safer in their environment. They often feel tense, worried, and anxious, but are unable to articulate exactly why they feel this way. Many anxious individuals are very uncertain of themselves in even minor stress producing situations, and they may have real difficulties in concentrating because of their high anxiety levels.

Other symptoms may include strong anxiety reactions with difficulty catching one's breath, perspiration, increased heart beat, dizziness, and feeling that they are dying. They may come to the Emergency Room of a hospital complaining of a heart attack or heart troubles. It is important to keep in mind that many elements of the anxiety reaction are seen in patients with other neurotic disorders.

Conversion Reactions or *Hysteria* involve the loss of ability to perform some physical function that the person could previously perform, which is psychogenic in origin. This reaction is an attempt by the individual to defend herself or himself from some anxiety producing situation by developing physical symptoms that have no organic or physical cause. These reactions are not common, and constitute less than five percent of neurotic disorders. The lost function is often symbolically related to a situation which has produced stress or anxiety, and is often an attempt to escape from that situation. The person may lose the ability to hear or speak, have unusual bodily sensations, or lose control of some motor function. Since there is no physical cause of dysfunction, some people assume that the pain or paralysis is not real, or that this type of person is faking. *Dissociative Reactions* also serve to protect the individual from particularly stressful situations. Amnesia, fugue, and multiple personalities are the major categories of dissociative reactions. Despite the prevalence of *amnesia* on soap operas, dissociative reactions account for less than five percent of all neurotic disorders. Amnesiacs usually forget specific information for a specified but variable period of time. The patient does not, however, forget his or her basic lifestyle or habits. In *fugue,* the person combines the amnesia with flight, and leaves the area where the stressful situation is. Usually the person is unaware of where he or she has been, or where he or she is going. There are very few cases of *multiple personalities.* In this disorder, the person shows different ways of responding to the environment. Each individual personality within the person is a complete personality system, and may dominate the person's reactions to his or her environment, depending upon the situation.

Obsessive-Compulsive Reactions involve either the inability to stop thinking about something the person does not want to think about, or the obligatory performance of a repetitive act. People experiencing these reactions often recognize they are irrational, but are unable to stop doing them. They often attempt to rearrange their environment, which they may perceive as threatening, in an attempt to impose control and structure, so they can control their environment and feel safer. Those suffering from compulsive reactions feel a strong need to perform or repeat certain behaviors, often in order to prevent something terrible from happening to them. (This might involve pre-determined ways to enter a room, brush their teeth, get into bed, begin conversations, etc.) Of course, many people may exhibit aspects of this behavior. Observing some professional baseball players before they pitch or take a pitch can certainly demonstrate this point. There is little cause for concern if the patterns are relatively temporary and help the person in some way obtain their goal. When the behaviors begin to unduly restrict a person's activities, then the situation becomes more serious. People exhibiting this behavior are often unable to make decisions effectively, are often perfectionists, have a strong need for structure, and are fairly rigid. Those who are obsessed with unwanted thoughts may have quite a variety of areas that they think about. The most common areas, however, concern religion, ethical concerns (something being absolutely right or wrong), bodily functions, and suicide.

Phobic Reactions involve a strong, persistent irrational fear of an object, condition, or place. It is believed that phobias usually involve a displacement of anxiety from the original cause to the phobic object. The phobia serves to assist the individual in avoiding the anxiety-causing situation. Some of the most common phobias include fear of crowds, being alone, darkness, thunderstorms, and high places. It is often very difficult to discover the symbolic significance of a particular phobia.

Neurotic Depressive Reactions involve an intensification of normal grief reactions. Research has indicated that those suffering from this reaction are unable to *bounce back* from upsetting or discouraging events. People who suffer from this reaction tend to have a poor self-concept, exaggerated dependency needs, a tendency to feel guilty about almost anything, and to turn those guilt feelings against themselves in a highly punitive way. The possibility of suicide should be kept in mind when working with these patients.

Categories of Psychosis

Psychoses are generally divided into two categories, *functional psychoses* and *organic psychoses*. Functional psychoses are caused by psychological stress, while organic psychoses are caused by a disorder of the brain for which physical pathology can be demonstrated. A third category, *toxic psychoses,* is sometimes used to refer to psychotic reactions caused by toxic substances such as drugs or poisons.

Schizophrenia accounts for approximately 25 percent of all first admissions to mental institutions, and is the largest single diagnostic group of psychotic patients. The *paranoid schizophrenic* shows a great deal of suspiciousness and hostility, and may be very aggressive. The *simple type schizophrenic* is shy and withdrawn, and shows interest in his or her environment. The *hebephrenic schizophrenic* often has bizarre mannerisms and may appear quite manic. He or she may laugh and giggle inappropriately, and become preoccupied with unimportant matters. The *catatonic schizophrenic* may remain motionless for days or hours, and may refuse to eat. The two phases of catatonia are the *stuporous phase* where the person is motionless and *catatonic excitement* where the person is over-active and appears manic. While the catatonic schizophrenic may alternate between these two phases, most show a preference for just one. Someone suffering from *schizoaffective schizophrenia* will have significant thought disorders and mood variations. They may initially appear to be depressed or manic, but a basic personality disorganization also exists. These are the major categories of schizophrenia you should need for the exam. Since the exam announcement states basic knowledge is required, it is very possible some of the above categories may be too specific. We have included them just in case, however.

The general symptoms of schizophrenia include an inability to deal with reality, the presence of hallucinations or delusions, inappropriate emotions, autism and various other unusual behaviors. There is often a very noticeable inability to organize thoughts. Schizophrenic reactions that occur suddenly are referred to as *acute* schizophrenic reactions, while those that develop slowly over a rather lengthy period are called *chronic* schizophrenic reactions.

Paranoid Reactions in people account for less than one percent of psychiatric admissions. Those with this behavior usually mistrust the motives of everyone, are very resentful, and often hostile. They may show signs of grandiosity or persecution. The person often believes that whatever happens is related to him or her. The major difference between paranoid patients and paranoid schizophrenics is that the paranoid patient usually has better control of his or her thought processes, and is able to make more appropriate responses to situations. They are usually more reality-oriented, and able to state their feelings more effectively.

Affective Reactions are those that represent a change in the normal affect, or mood, of a person. There are two major categories of affective disorders: *manic-depressive reactions* and *involutional psychotic reactions.* In the manic-depressive reaction, the manic and depressive states alternate. In the manic phase, the person may be extremely talkative, agitated or elated, and demonstrate a great deal of physical and verbal activity. They may also exhibit some grandiosity. In the depressive phase, the person is joyless, quiet, and inhibited. The manic reactions are often divided into three degress of severity, each category representing a more severe degree of manic reaction. *Hypomania* is the least severe, *acute mania* is the next, and *delirious mania* is the most severe state. The term *involutional psychosis is* usually related to a patient's age. For women, the involutional age is considered to be somewhere between 40 and 55, and the involutional period for men is somewhere between 50 and 65. It seems that stresses are greater for men and women during these periods, and that these stresses may trigger psychotic reactions which are generally transient. These people generally have a long history of feeling guilty and very anxious, have little diversity of activity, and few sources of satisfaction in their lives.

Selected Personality Disorders

This category includes behavior which is maladaptive, but neither psychotic nor neurotic. This group includes *antisocial reactions*, the *abuse of alchol and other drugs,* and *sexual deviations*. The *antisocial* or *sociopathic* personality type fails to develop a concern for others and uses relationships to get what he or she wants. There is little or no concern about what effect their behavior might have on others, and they seldom feel remorse or guilt. They are often likable, friendly, intelligent people. Their relationships with others tend to be superficial, however, because they lack the capacity for deep emotional responses. The sociopath is often impulsive and seeks immediate gratification of his or her wants. He or she often is unreliable, untruthful, undependable and insincere. A large number of people have sociopathic traits which, as with most other characteristics, vary in severity and number. Sociopaths are found in all professions, although many are able to control their acting out behaviors or channel them in more socially acceptable ways. They avoid acting out not because of internal values, but because they do not wish to get caught. Sociopaths usually have a low frustration tolerance, are easily bored, and continually seek excitement. The sociopath most frequently comes to treatment because he or she has been *caught* doing something or been required to seek help by an employer or family member.

Sexual Deviations occur in those who fail to develop what their society considers appropriate sexual behavior. The major sexual deviations include child molestation, rape, sadism, masochism, voyeurism, fetishism, transvestism, exhibitionism, pedophilia, and incest. As you can see, some of these behaviors are much more harmful to other people than others are.

PSYCHOTROPIC DRUGS (REACTIONS AND USES)

The two major classifications of the psychotropic drugs are the tranquilizers, which are further divided into major (or anti-psychotic) and minor (or antianxiety) groups, and the antidepressants. Other drugs used include anticonvulsants, sedatives, hypnotics, and antiparkinsons.

Tranquilizers are meant to calm disturbed patients, and free them from agitation or disturbance. Drugs designed as *antipsychotic,* or *major tranquilizers,* also help to reduce the frequency of hallucinations, delusions, thought disorders, and the type of withdrawal seen in catatonic schizophrenia. It may take several days of drug therapy before the symptoms begin to subside, but during this time the patient becomes less fearful, hostile and upset by his disturbed sensory perceptions. The *phenothiazine derivatives* are the largest group of antipsychotic drugs. All the drugs in this group have essentially the same type of action on the body, but vary according to strength and the type and severity of their side effects. These drugs include:

Thorazine	Trilafon	Taractan
Mellaril	Compazine	Navane
Stelazine	Dartal	Sordinal
Prolixin	Proketazine	Haldol
Sparine	Tindal	Loxitane
Vesprin	Repoise	Moban

Serious side effects are very important to watch for. For these drugs, the phenothiazine derivatives, there are three major types of extrapyramidal symptoms (EPS): (1) akinesia - inability to sit still, complaints of fatigue and weakness, and continuous movement of the hands, mouth, and body; (2) pseudoparkinsonism -restlessness, mask-like facial expressions, drooling, and tremors; (3) tardive dyskenesia - lack of control over voluntary movements. Symptoms may include involuntary grimacing, sucking and chewing movements, pursing of the tongue and mouth, jerking of the hands, feet and neck, and drooping head. Immediate action must be taken to combat these side effects. The administration of antiparkinson drugs usually produces a dramatic reduction in symptoms. Unless spotted and treated early, however, these can become permanent.

Other side effects may include muscle spasms, shuffling gait, skin rash, eye problems, trembling hands and fingers, fainting, wormlike tongue movements, sore throat and fever, yellowing of skin or eyes, dry mouth, constipation, excessive weight gain, edema, a drop in blood pressure when moving from a lying to standing position, decreased sexual interest, sensitivity to light and prone to sunburn and visual problems, blurred vision, drowsiness, and increased perspiration. Just about any physical symptom or behavior could be caused by a reaction to a drug.

Special Considerations: Patients receiving a high dose of a phenothiazine drug should have their blood pressure checked regularly. Long exposures of skin to sunlight should be avoided (a wide-brimmed hat and long-sleeved clothing can also help). If a patient receiving phenothiazines is lethargic and wants to sleep a great deal, the dose of the drug may be too high and need adjustment. Patients on phenothiazines should not drive or use dangerous equipment. These drugs greatly increase the effects of alcohol. In the first three to five days, a person may feel drowsy and dizzy upon standing. Antipsychotic drugs tend to mask the symptoms of diseases and dictate that patients receiving them undergo thorough physical examinations every six months.

The *Minor Tranquilizers*, or *antianxiety drugs*, reduce anxiety and muscle tension associated with it. They are useful primarily with psychoneurotic and psychosomatic disorders. When given in small doses, they are relatively safe and have few side effects. Unlike the antipsychotic drugs, some of the antianxiety drugs tend to be habit-forming. If the drug is discontinued, the person may experience severe withdrawal symptoms, such as convulsions or delirium. These drugs include:

Librium	Milpath	Frienquel
Azene	Deprol	Phobex
Tranxene	Milprem	Softran
Valium	Miltown	Atarax
Ativan	Robaxin	Vistaril
Serax	Solacen	Trancopal

Side effects may include rashes, chills, fever, nausea, headaches, poor muscle coordination, some inability to concentrate, and dizziness. Excessive amounts of these drugs may lead to coma and death; however, death is less likely with an overdose of minor tranquilizers than with an overdose of barbituates. Patients taking these should be cautioned against driving or performing tasks that require careful attention to detail and mental alertness.

Antidepressants, such as the *Tricyclic Antidepressants*, are used to elevate the patient's mood, and increase appetite and mental and physical alertness. Drugs in this group tend to take one to four weeks of use before significant changes occur in the patient's outlook. Since these drugs sometimes excite patients instead of sedating them, patients must be observed closely for reactions. These drugs include:

Elavil	Sinequan
Endep	Tofranil
Asendine	Aventyl
Morpramin	Vivactil
Adapin	Marplan
Presamine	Janimine

Common side effects include dry mouth, fatigue, weakness, nausea, increased appetite, increased perspiration, heartburn, and sensitivity to sunlight. *Serious side effects* include blurred vision, constipation, irregular heartbeat, problems urinating, headache, eye pain, fainting, hallucination, vomiting, unusually slow pulse, seizures, skin rash, sore throat and fever, and yellowing of eyes and skin.

Serious side effects include blurred vision, constipation, irregular heartbeat, problems urinating, headache, eye pain, fainting, hallucination, vomiting, unusually slow pulse, seizures, skin rash, sore throat and fever, and yellowing of eyes and skin.

Monoamineoxidose Inhibitors (MAO Inhibitors) are sometimes used for depression, but can have *very* serious side effects, and can also lead to serious hypertensive crisis. Their use must be very closely monitored. Their use with some over-the-counter drugs can be very serious. Foods containing Typtophen or Tyramine (some examples: caffeine, chocolate, herring, beans, chicken liver, cheese, beer, pickles, wine) should be avoided also. *Side effects* to watch for include severe headaches, stiff neck, nausea, vomiting, dilated pupils, and cold, clammy skin. A hypertensive crisis requires *immediate* treatment. These drugs include: Marplan, Nardil, Parnate, and Ludiomil.

In addition to the above psychotropic drugs, sedatives, hypnotics, anticonvulsants, and antiparkinsons drugs are also used. Since the exam announcement includes uses and reactions of only the psychotropic drugs, we will not review the non-psychotropic drugs. We will mention, however, the use and reactions of *Lithium Carbonate* (also known as Eskolith, Lithane,

Lithobid, and Lithonate). This drug is primarily used in the treatment of manic depressive psychoses since it is effective in decreasing excessive motor activity, talking, and unstable behavior by acting on the brain's metabolism. It also decreases swings in mood. The correct dose is close to the overdose level for this drug, so it is important to watch closely for symptoms and to report them immediately. *Common side effects* include dry mouth, metal taste, slightly increased urination, hand tremors, increased appetite, and fatigue. *Serious side effects* include greatly increased urination, nausea, vomiting, diarrhea, loss of muscle coordination, muscle cramps or weakness, irritability, confusion, slurred speech, blackout spells, and coma. These side effects require medical attention. *Special Considerations:* This drug must sometimes be taken from one to several weeks before the resident feels better. Hot weather, hot baths, and too much exercise can be dangerous, as too much perspiring can lead to an overdose. The person should drink two to three quarts of fluid a day, but should not drink large quantities of caffeine-containing beverages like coffee, tea, or colas.

GLOSSARY OF BASIC PSYCHIATRIC TERMS

TABLE OF CONTENTS

	Page
Accident Prone ... Anxiety	1
Anxiety Reaction (Anxiety Neurosis) ... Catatonic State	2
Character Disorder ... Conversion	3
Conversion Reaction ... Depression	4
Disorientation ... Environment	5
Epilepsy ... Free Association	6
Frustration ... Hypnosis (Hypnotic Trance)	7
Hypochondriasis ... Insight	8
Instinct ... Looseness of Association	9
Maladjustment ... Mind	10
Motivation ... Object	11
Obsession ... Paranoid State	12
Pathogenesis ... Projective Tests	13
Psyche ... Psychosomatic	14
Psychosurgery ... Reversal	15
Sadism ... Stress	16
Subject ... Turning Against the Self	17
Unconscious ... Waxy Flexibility	18

GLOSSARY OF BASIC PSYCHIATRIC TERMS

A

ACCIDENT PRONE
    Special susceptibility to accidents due to psychological causes.

ADDICTION
    A descriptive name for a type of psychiatric illness (character disorder) characterized by excessive psychological and/or physiologic dependence upon the intake of some substance, as, for example, alcohol or an opiate.

ADJUSTMENT
    The series of technics or processes by which the individual strives to meet the continuous changes that take place within himself and in his environment. Synonym: adaptation. (Some authorities consider adjustment to refer particularly to psychological activity and adaptation to physiologic activity.)

AFFECT
    Generalized feeling tone. (Usually considered to be more persistent than emotion and less so than mood.)
    Affective, pertaining to affect.
    Affective psychosis, a psychosis characterized by an extreme alteration in mood in the direction of mania or of depression.

AGGRESSION (Aggressive Drive)
    A term used in various ways; in the usq.ge of psychiatry, an instinct-like force, much influenced by early experience, motivating the individual to destructive activity.

AIM
    Intention or purpose; in psychiatric literature the term is used chiefly in the discussion of instincts; the *aim* of an instinctual drive may be defined as an action on the part of the individual that involves the *object* of the drive and results in gratification. Thus, the aim of the instinctual drive, hunger, is eating.

AMBIVALENCE
    The experiencing of contradictory strivings or emotions toward an object or situation. In extreme form, characteristic of *schizophrenia.*

ANAL CHARACTER (PERSONALITY)
    (1) In psychoanalysis a pattern of behavior in an adult that originates in the anal eroticism of infancy and is characterized by such traits as excessive orderliness, miserliness, and obstinacy.
    (2) A type of character (personality) disorder in which many of the individual's conflicts and defenses remain those appropriate to the muscle-training period, usually characterized by such traits as parsimony, rigidity, and pedantry.

ANAL PERIOD
    One of the developmental stages; the muscle-training period.

ANTHROPOLOGY
    The science of man or mankind in the widest sense; the history of human society; the developmental aspects of man as a species.

ANXIETY
    (1) Apprehension, the source of which is largely unknown or unrecognized. It is different from fear, which is the emotional response to a consciously recognized and usually external danger.
    (2) A state of tension and distress akin to fear, but produced by the threatened loss of inner control rather than by an external danger.

Anxiety attack, a phenomenon characterized by intense feelings of anxiety plus such physiologic manifestations as increased pulse and respiratory rates and increased perspiration.

ANXIETY REACTION (ANXIETY NEUROSIS)

A *psychoneurosis* characterized by the more or less continuous presence of anxiety in excess of normal and occasional clear-cut *anxiety attacks.*

ATTITUDE

One's physical and emotional position and manner with respect to another person, thing, or situation.

Attitude therapy, a method of treatment utilizing the assumption by the personnel of attitudes calculated to exert a favorable effect upon the patient.

AUTISM

Self-preoccupation with loss of interest in and appreciation of other persons and socially accepted behavior. *Autistic thinking,* thought processes determined by inner needs and relatively uninfluenced by environmental considerations, a characteristic of *schizophrenia.*

AUTISTIC CHILD

In child psychiatry, a child who responds chiefly to inner thoughts who does not relate to his environment, and whose overall functioning is immature and often appears retarded.

B

BASIC DRIVE

In human psychology, one of a group of hereditarily transmitted motivating forces, deriving ultimately from biochemical changes within the organism; used synonymously with instinct.

BEHAVIOR (HUMAN)

All the activity of a human being that is capable of observation by another person.

BEHAVIOR DISORDER

See Personality Disorder.

BLOCKING

(1) Difficulty in recollection, or interruption of a train of thought or speech, caused by unconscious emotional factors.

(2) An involuntary, functional interference with a person's thinking, memory or communication. (Usually the term is employed with reference to a psychotherapeutic situation.)

C

CASTRATION

Literally, the removal or the destruction of the gonads (ovaries or testes). In psychoanalytic terminology, the loss of the penis.

CASTRATION ANXIETY

Anxiety due to danger (fantasied) of loss of the genitals or injuries to them. May be precipitated by everyday events that have symbolic significance and appear to be threatening, such as loss of job, loss of a tooth, or an experience of ricidule or humiliation.

CATALEPSY

A condition usually characterized by trance-like states. May occur in organic or psychological disorders or under hypnosis.

CATATONIC STATE (Catatonia)

(1) A state characterized by immobility with, muscular rigidity or inflexibility and at times by excitability. Virtually always a symptom of schizophrenia.

(2) One of the four classic schizophrenic subgroups (syndromes), usually beginning at a

relatively early age and characterized by a rapid onset and interference with normal motor function.

CHARACTER DISORDER
See Personality Disorder.

COMPENSATION
(1) A defense mechanism, operating unconsciously, by which the individual attempts to make up for (i.e., to compensate for) real or fancied deficiencies.
(2) A conscious process in which the individual strives to make up for real or imagined defects in such areas as physique, performance, skills, or psychological attributes.

COMPLEX
(1) A group of associated ideas that have a common emotional tie. These are largely unconscious and significantly influence attitudes and associations. Examples are:

Inferiority Complex - Feelings of inferiority stemming from real or imagined physical or social inadequacies that may cause anxiety or other adverse reactions. The individual may overcompensate by excessive ambition or by the development of special skills, often in the very field in which he was originally handicapped.

Oedipus Complex - Attachment of the child for the parent of the opposite sex, accompanied by envious and aggressive feelings toward the parent of the same sex. These feelings are largely repressed (i.e., made unconscious) because of the fear of displeasure or punishment by the parent of the same sex. In its original use, the term applied only to the male child.

(2) In psychoanalytic terminology, a group of associated ideas and feelings that, though unconscious, influence the subject's conscious attitudes and behavior.

COMPULSION
(1) An insistent, repetitive, and unwanted urge to perform an act that is contrary to the person's ordinary conscious wishes or standards. Failure to perform the compulsive act results in overt anxiety.
(2) An act that is carried out, in some degree, against the subject's conscious wishes, either to avoid the anxiety that would otherwise appear, or to dispel a disturbing *obsession.*
compulsive, pertaining to a compulsion.

COMPULSIVE PERSONALITY
A type of personality disorder; more specifically, a type of neurotic personality. *See* Anal Character (Personality).

CONFLICT
A struggle between two or more opposing forces. *Intrapersonal* (*intrapsychic; conflict,* a struggle between forces within a single personality. *Interpersonal conflict,* a struggle between two or more individuals.

CONGENITAL
Present from birth; mayor may not be hereditary.

CONSCIENCE
Equivalent to the conscious portion of the superego; in strict psychoanalytic terminology, the "ego ideal."

CONSCIOUS
Aware or sensible; "mentally awake."

CONVERSION
Sensory or motor dysfunctions by which the subject gives symbolic expression to a conflict (of which he is not conscious).

CONVERSION REACTION

A psychoneurosis, formerly called "conversion hysteria," characterized by conversions.

CULTURE

The characteristic attainments of a people.

CYCLOTHYMIA

A tendency or a proneness to repeated, exaggerated, largely irrational alterations in mood, usually between euphoria and depression.

Cyclothymic, pertaining to cyclothymia.

Cyclothymia personality, a type of psychotic personality disorder, often the precursor of manic-depressive psychosis.

D

DEATH INSTINCT (Thanatos)

In Freudian theory, the unconscious drive toward dissolution and death. Coexists with and is in opposition to the life instinct (Eros).

DEFENSE MECHANISM

(1) A specific process, operating unconsciously, that is employed to seek relief from emotional conflict and freedom from anxiety.

(2) A psychological technic performed by the ego but carried out below the subject's threshold of awareness, designed to ward off anxiety or unpleasant tensions.

DELIRIUM

An altered level of consciousness (awareness), often acute and in most instances reversible, manifested by disorientation and confusion and induced by an interference with the metabolic processes of the neurons of the brain. *Delirium tremens,* an agitated delirious state occurring as a complication of chronic alcoholism.

DELUSION

A fixed idea, arising out of the subject's inner needs and contrary to the observed facts as these are interpreted by normal persons under the same circumstances; a symptom of psychosis.

DEMENTIA

A chronic, typically irreversible deterioration of intellectual capacities, due to organic disease of the brain that has produced structural changes (the actual death of neurons).

Dementia paralytica, formerly "paresis," a chronic syphilitic inflammation of the brain and its membranous coverings resulting, if untreated, in progressive dementia and paralysis and ultimately in death.

Dementia praecox, an old (obsolescent) (and misleading) term for schizophrenia.

DENIAL

A *defense mechanism* in which the ego refuses to allow awareness of some aspect of reality.

DEPRESSION

(1) Psychiatrically, a morbid sadness, dejection, or melancholy; to be differentiated from grief, which is realistic and proportionate to what has been lost. A depression may be a symptom of any psychiatric disorder or may constitute its principal manifestation.

(2) A pathologic state brought on by feelings of loss and/or guilt and characterized by sadness and a lowering of self-esteem.

Neurotic depressive reaction, a state of depression of neurotic intensity in which *reality-testing* is largely unimpaired and in which physiologic disturbances, if present, are usually mild.

Psychotic depressive reaction, a state of depression of psychotic intensity in which reality-testing is severely impaired and in which physiologic disturbances *(vegetative signs)* are usually conspicuous.

Reactive depression, a state of depression -- intensity not specified -- for which the precipitating stress can be clearly discerned and seen to be of some magnitude.

DISORIENTATION

Confusion of the subject with respect to such information as the correct time and place, a knowledge of his personal identity and an understanding of his situation; typically seen in *delirium* and *dementia.*

DISPLACEMENT

A general term for a group of psychological phenomena (technics) in which certain strivings or feelings are (unconsciously) transferred from one object, activity, or situation to another (which acquires a similar meaning). The defense technic of sublimation is one example of a successful displacement.

DISSOCIATION

A breaking of psychic connections, of associations.

DISSOCIATIVE REACTION

Formerly called "hysterical amnesia." A psychoneurosis in which a group of thoughts, feelings and memories becomes separated from the rest of the personality.

DRIVE

See Basic Drive.

DYNAMIC (PSYCHODYNAMIC)

Pertaining to the forces operating within the personality and determining the behavior, particularly unconscious forces. Dynamic psychiatry, a psychiatry concerned with the understanding of such motivating forces.

E

EGO

(1) In psychoanalytic theory, one of the three major divisions of human personality, the others being the id and superego. The ego, commonly identified with consciousness of self, is the mental agent mediating among three contending forces: the external demands of social pressure or reality; the primitive instinctual demands arising from the id imbedded as it is in the deepest level of the unconscious; and the claims of the superego, born of parental and social prohibitions and functioning as an internal censor or "conscience."

(2) One of the three agencies or aspects of the mind, the ego is the aspect that is in contact with the environment through the sensory apparatus, that appriases environmental and inner changes and that directs behavior through its control of the motor apparatus.

ELECTROCONVULSIVE THERAPY (E.C.T., ELECTROSHOCK THERAPY)

A method of treatment of psychiatric disorders by passing an electric current through the brain, producing an artificial seizure.

ELECTROENCEPHALOGRAPH

An instrument, based on the string galvanometer, for measuring very small changes in potential derived from the electrical activity of the neurons of the brain. *Electroencephalogram,* the record obtained with the electroencephalograph, a "brain-wave tracing."

EMPATHY

(1) An objective awareness of the feelings, emotions, and behavior of another person. To be distinguished from sympathy, which is usually nonobjective and noncritical.

(2) A deep recognition of the significance of another person's behavior, which retains a certain objectivity and yet involves intellectual, emotional and motivational experiences corresponding to those of the other person.

ENVIRONMENT

All that surrounds the individual, including living and non-living, material and immaterial elements.

EPILEPSY

A disorder characterized by periodic seizures, and sometimes accompanied by a loss of consciousness. May be caused by organic or emotional disturbances.

Major epilepsy (grand mal) - Characterized by gross convulsive seizures, with loss of consciousness.

Minor epilepsy (petit mal) - Minor nonconvulsive epileptic seizures; may be limited to only momentary lapses of consciousness.

ETHOLOGY

The scientific study of the instincts. *Ethologist,* one who makes a scientific study of the instincts.

ETIOLOGY

Pertaining to causation; in medicine and nursing, pertaining to the causation of disease.

EUPHORIA

(1) An exaggerated feeling of physical and emotional well-being inconsonant with reality.

(2) An exaggerated (unrealistic) sense of well-being.

EXHIBITIONISM

Erotic pleasure in exposing the body to the view of others; in adults, a form of perversion when it is the principal form of erotic expression.

EXTROVERSION

A state in which attention and energies are largely directed outward from the self, as opposed to interest primarily directed toward the self, as in introversion.

F

FACULTY

A power or a function, especially a mental one.

FAMILY TRIANGLE

The situation, involving the child and the parents, in which the child experiences the wish to displace the parent of the same sex and possess the parent of the opposite sex. Family-triangle period, a developmental phase characterized by maximum intensity of these strivings. Synonymous with *Oedipal period*.

FANTASY (PHANTASY)

An image -- conscious or unconscious -- formed by recombinations of memories and interpretations of them.

FEAR

An experience, having both psychological and physiologic components, stimulated by the awareness of impending danger in the environment.

FIXATION

The persistence into later life of interests and behavior patterns appropriate to an earlier developmental phase.

FLATNESS OF AFFECT

A lack of normal emotional responsiveness, especially characteristic of *schizophrenia*.

FLIGHT OF IDEAS

A morbid type of thought sequence manifested through speech, characterized by its rapidity and by numerous and sudden shifts in topics, but that tends to be comprehensible to the normal observer. Typical of mania.

FREE ASSOCIATION

(1) In psychoanalytic therapy, spontaneous, uncensored verbalization by the patient of whatever comes to mind.

(2) A technic, used in *psychoanalysis,* in which the patient reports verbally his thoughts, emotions and sensations in whatever order they occur, making no effort at deliberate organization, censorship, or control.

FRUSTRATION

A blocking or nongratification of needs.

FUGUE

A major state of personality dissociation characterized by amnesia and actual physical flight from the immediate environment.

FUNCTIONAL

Pertaining solely or primarily to function. *Functional psychosis,* a psychosis occurring on the basis of disturbed mental functioning in the absence of structural brain damage.

G

GARRULOUSNESS

Excessive talkativeness, especially about trivial things.

GENITAL PHASE (OF DEVELOPMENT)

In psychoanalytic terminology, a synonym for emotional maturity.

GROUP

Any two or more persons who are set off from others, either temporarily or permanently, by a special type of association (relationship), as, for example, an important common interest.

Group therapy, a form of *psychotherapy* taking place among a group of patients under the guidance of a therapist.

H

HALLUCINATION

A sensory experience, occurring (in the absence of adequate reality-testing) on the basis of the subject's inner needs and independently of stimulation from the environment.

HALLUCINOGEN

A chemical substance capable of inducing hallucinations.

HEBEPHRENIA

One of the classic schizophrenic subgroups, the one having the most ominous prognosis. *Hebephrenic schizophrenia* is a synonym.

HEREDITARY

Genetically transmitted from parent to offspring.

HETEROSEXUAL

Pertaining to the opposite sex.

HOMEOSTASIS

A tendency to uniformity and stability in the normal body states of the organism (Walter B. Cannon).

HOMOSEXUAL

(adj.) Pertaining to an erotic interest in members of one's own sex. (noun) One having an erotic interest in members of his own sex.

(1) Sexual attraction or relationship between members of the same sex.

Latent homosexuality - A condition characterized by unconscious homosexual desires.

Overt homosexuality - Homosexuality that is consciously recognized or practiced.

(2) *Homosexuality,* a condition characterized by the subject's having an erotic interest in members of his own sex, a form of *personality disorder.*

HYPNOSIS (HYPNOTIC TRANCE)

(1) A state of increased receptivity to suggestion and direction, initially induced by the

influence of another person. The degree may vary from mild suggestibility to a trance state so profound as to be used in surgical operations.

    (2) An artificially induced state, akin to sleep, in which the subject enters into so close a relationship with the hypnotist that the suggestions of the latter become virtually indistinguishable from the activity of his own ego.

HYPOCHONDRIASIS
    (1) Overconcern with the state of physical or emotional health, accompanied by various bodily complaints without demonstrable organic pathology.

    (2) A severe type of *psychoneurosis*, characterized by a morbid preoccupation with one's body and a partial withdrawal of interest from the environment. *Hypochondriac*, one afflicted with hypochondriasis.

HYSTERIA
A *psychoneurosis*; the older term for the conditions now designated as *conversion reaction* and *dissociative reaction*.

HYSTERICAL PERSONALITY
(1) A personality type characterized by shifting emotional feelings, susceptibility to suggestion, impulsive behavior, attention seeking, immaturity, and self-absorption; not necessarily disabling.

(2) A form of *personality disorder (neurotic personality)* characterized by conflicts and defenses similar to those found in persons with hysteria.
Hysteric, one afflicted with hysteria.

I

ID
The one of the three agencies or aspects of the mind that contains the psychic representations of the instinctual drives.

IDEATION
The process of forming ideas.

IDENTIFICATION
The adoption -- unconsciously -- of some of the characteristics of another person. Strictly speaking, the term refers to the result of the defense mechanism of *introjection*. (Sometimes identification and introjection are used loosely as synonyms.)

ILLUSION
A false perceptual experience occurring in response to an environmental stimulus; usually a symptom of serious mental illness.

INCEST
Culturally prohibited sexual relations between members of a family, usually persons closely related by blood, as father and daughter, mother and son, or brother and sister. INHIBITION

    (1) Interference with or restriction of activities; the result of an unconscious defense against forbidden instinctual drives.

    (2) The restraining or the stopping of a process; in psychiatry, the term usually refers to an inner force that opposes the gratification of a basic drive.

INSANITY
Now a term of legal or medicolegal significance only, referring to a mental disorder of sufficient gravity to bring the subject under special legal restrictions and immunities.

INSIGHT
    (1) Self-understanding. A major goal of psychotherapy. The extent of the individual's understanding of the origin, nature, and mechanisms of his attitudes and behavior.

    (2) In the broad psychiatric sense, the patient's knowledge that he suffers from an emo-

tional illness; in the narrow psychiatric sense, the patient's knowledge of the specific, hitherto unconscious, meaning of his symptom(s) or of some other aspect of illness.

INSTINCT

A term of many meanings; in dynamic psychiatric usage it is usually considered as synonymous with *basic drive.*

INSULIN COMA THERAPY

A method of treatment of psychoses through the induction of a series of comas by means of insulin injections.

INTERNALIZE

To place within (the mind). Said of a conflict or a state of tension that, in its original form, existed between an individual and some aspect of his environment, but that has come to exist within the mind (i.e., between one aspect of the personality and another). Thus *anxiety* is often found to be an *internalized fear.*

INTERPERSONAL

Existing between two or more individuals; often contrasted with intrapersonal.

INTERPRETATION

A scientific guess, made by a psychotherapist about a patient, explaining some aspect of the latter's thoughts, feelings or behavior.

INTRAPERSONAL (INTRAPSYCHIC)

Existing within a mind or a personality; often contrasted with *interpersonal.*

INTROJECTION

One of the *defense mechanisms;* the psychological process whereby a quality or an attribute of another person is taken into and made a part of the subject's personality (unconsciously). Often used loosely as synonymous with *identification.*

INVOLUTION (INVOLUTIONAL PERIOD)

A period in late middle age in which retrogressive physiologic changes take place, causing a loss of the capacity for reproduction. *Involutional psychosis,* a psychosis for which a major precipitating factor has been the advent of involution.

ISOLATION

One of the *defense mechanisms;* the psychological process whereby the actual facts of an experience are allowed to remain in consciousness, but the linkage between these facts and the related emotions or impulses is broken.

L

LATENCY (LATENCY PERIOD)

One of the phases of human development, occurring between the *family-triangle period* and *puberty* (approximately, ages 6 to 11 or 12 years), characterized by a relative instinctual quiescence coupled with a rapid intellectual development.

LEVELS OF AWARENESS (LEVELS OF CONSCIOUSNESS)

An expression referring to the fact that mental activity takes place with varying degrees of the subject's awareness: an individual may be entirely unaware, dimly aware, or fully aware of a given bit of mental activity.

LIBIDO

An inclusive term for the sexual-social drives.

LOBOTOMY (PREFRONTAL)

A psychosurgical procedure in which certain tracts of the brain are severed, thus stopping the interaction between the prefrontal areas (of the cerebral cortex) and the rest of the brain. Sometimes used as a therapeutic measure in severe psychoses.

LOOSENESS OF ASSOCIATION

A symptom of serious mental illness, usually of *schizophrenia,* in which the logical connections between a patient's successive thoughts are absent or are not discernible to the observer.

M

MALADJUSTMENT
A state of disequilibrium between the individual and his environment, in which his needs are not being gratified.

MALINGER
To feign an illness.
Malingerer, one who feigns an illness.

MANIA
(1) A suffix denoting a pathological preoccupation with some desire, idea, or activity; a morbid compulsion. Some frequently encountered manias are: *dipsomania,* compulsion to drink alcoholic beverages; *egomania,* pathological preoccupation with self; *kleptomania,* compulsion to steal; *megalomania,* pathological preoccupation with delusions of power or wealth; *monomania,* pathological preoccupation with one subject; *necromania,* pathological preoccupation with the dead; pyromania, morbid compulsion to set fires.
(2) A morbid state of extreme euphoria and excitement with loss of reality-testing; one of the phases of *manic-depressive psychosis.*
Manic (adj.), pertaining to mania; (noun), one who suffers from mania.

MANIC-DEPRESSIVE REACTION
A group of psychiatric disorders marked by conspicuous mood swings, ranging from normal to elation or to depression, or alternating. Officially regarded as a psychosis but may also exist in milder form.
Depressed phase - Characterized by depression of mood with retardation and inhibition of thinking and physical activity.
Manic phase - Characterized by depression of mood with retardation of thought, speech, and bodily motion, and by elation or grandiosity of mood, and irritability.

MASOCHISM
(1) Pleasure derived from undergoing physical or psychological pain inflicted by oneself or by others. It may be consciously sought or unconsciously arranged or invited. Present to some degree in all human relations and to greater degrees in all psychiatric disorders. It is the converse of sadism, in which pain is inflicted on another, and the two tend to coexist in the same individual.
(2) Finding gratification in pain; in the narrow sense, one of the perversions.

MASTURBATION
Erotic stimulation of one's external genitalia.

MATURITY
The state of being fully adult; psychologically characterized particularly by the ability to love others in a relatively non-selfish way.

MECHANISM (MENTAL, DEFENSE)
See Defense Mechanism.

MILIEU
The total environment, emotional as well as physical.
Milieu therapy, treatment by means of controlled modifications of the patient's environment.

MIND
The body in action as a unit. *Mental,* pertaining to mind as thus defined. *Mental illness,* accurately speaking, any illness of the mind, regardless of severity; often incorrectly restricted to severe psychiatric conditions.

MOTIVATION
A psychological state that incites to action.
MOURNING
The process that follows upon the loss of a love object, through which the subject gradually frees himself from the disequilibrium caused by the loss.
MULTIPLE PERSONALITY
A morbid condition, related to *dissociative reaction,* in which the normal organization of the personality is split up into distinct portions, all having a fairly complex organization of their own. (If there are only two such portions, the term dual personality is used.)
MUSCLE-TRAINING PERIOD
One of the developmental stages, lasting from the end of *infancy* to the beginning of the *family-triangle period* (about age 1½ to age 3), during which the child receives training in sphincter control and other motor activities. Synonymous with *anal period.*
MYELIN
The fatlike substance that forms a sheath around the medullated nerve fibers. *Myelinization,* the process of acquiring a myelin sheath.

N

NARCISSISM (NARCISM)
(1) Self-love, as opposed to object-love (love of another person). Some degree of narcissism is considered healthy and normal, but an excess interferes with relations with others.
(2) Self-love; extreme narcissism is the emotional position found in the newborn infant and in certain psychoses. The term is derived from the Greek legend of Narcissus, a youth who fell in love with his own image.
Narcissistic, loving oneself excessively in a childish or an infantile fashion.
NARCOSYNTHESIS
A form of psychiatric treatment in which contact is established with the patient while he is under the influence of a hypnotic drug.
NEGATIVISM
A tendency to resist suggestions or requests, often accompanied by a response that is, in some sense, the opposite of the one sought. *Negativistic,* expressing negativism.
NEOLOGISM
A newly coined word, or the act of coining such a word; a phenomenon seen in *schizophrenia* and in some cases of *organic brain disease.*
NEURASTHENIA
One of the psychoneuroses, related to *anxiety reaction,* characterized by chronic feelings of fatigue and tension and often by disturbances in the sexual function and minor disturbances in the digestive function.
NEUROPHYSIOLOGY
The physiology of the nervous sytem. *Neurophysiologist,* a specialist in neurophysiology.
NEUROSIS
See psychoneurosis.

O

OBJECT
A term with several meanings. In the broadest sense, it is used in contrast with the term *subject* and means anything in the environment, including another person. In a narrower sense, *object* refers to "a satisfying something" in the environment that is capable of offering instinctual gratification. Thus, *love object* refers to a person toward whom the subject experiences libidinal strivings.

OBSESSION
- (1) Persistent, unwanted idea or impulse that cannot be eliminated by logic or reasoning.
- (2) A thought, recognized by the subject as more or less irrational, that persistently recurs, despite the subject's conscious wish to avoid or ignore it.

obsessive, pertaining to or afflicted with obsessions.

OBSESSIVE-COMPULSIVE NEUROSIS

One of the psychoneuroses, characterized by *obsessions* and *compulsions* and an underlying personality type whose conflicts involve problems of the muscle-training period.

OEDIPUS

A character in Greek legend, who unwittingly killed his father and married his mother and was subsequently punished by the gods by being blinded. *Oedipus complex,* a term referring to the erotic attachment of the (normal as well as neurotic) small child to the parent of the opposite sex, repressed largely because of the fear of bodily mutilation ("castration") by the presumedly jealous parent of the same sex. *Oedipal period,* same as *family-triangle period.*

ORAL PERIOD

The first postuterine developmental period, roughly synonymous with infancy, in which the individual's central experiences are those involved in the act of sucking.

ORAL PERSONALITY

One of the *personality disorders,* characterized by the persistence in adult life of problems and defenses appropriate to the *oral period* of development.

ORGANIC

Based on structural alterations, gross or microscopic. *Organic psychosis,* a psychosis the etiology of which involves structural damage. (The term also includes *toxic psychosis,* in which the physical alterations are at a submicroscopic -- i.e., chemical -- level.)

ORGANISM

A general term for any living creature, including man.

OVERCOMPENSATION

A conscious or unconscious process in which a real or fancied physical or psychological deficit inspires exaggerated correction.

OVERT

Discernible; "out in the open."

P

PANIC (PANIC REACTION)

A morbid state characterized by extreme fear and/or anxiety, causing a temporary disorganization of the personality.

PARANOIA

Traditionally considered to be one of the three major functional (nonorganic) psychoses, but now generally thought to be one variety of paranoid schizophrenia. A pathologic state, characterized by extreme suspiciousness and highly organized delusions of persecution, occurring in the presence of a clear sensorium and relatively appropriate affective responses.

Paranoid, pertaining to paranoia or paranoid schizophrenia.

Paranoid reaction, an acute, often self-limited state, resembling paranoia; the term is inclusive of paranoid syndromes arising on the basis of organic disease.

PARANOID SCHIZOPHRENIA

One of the four major schizophrenic subgroups, characterized by the usual features of *schizophrenia* plus delusions of persecution and/or grandeur (often loosely organized), auditory hallucinations in keeping with the delusions, and a marked, generalized suspiciousness.

PARANOID STATE

Characterized by delusions of persecution. A paranoid state may be of short duration or chronic.

PATHOGENESIS

The mode of development of disease states.

PERCEPTION

A psychological experience in which sensory stimuli are integrated to form an image (the significance of which is influenced by past experiences).

PERSONALITY

The whole group of adjustment technics and equipment that are characteristic for a given individual in meeting the various situations of life.

PERSONALITY DISORDER

In the limited (diagnostic) sense, a type of psychiatric illness in which the patient's inner difficulties are revealed, not by specific symptoms but by an unhealthy pattern of living. Thus used, roughly synonymous with *character disorder* and *behavior disorder*. In a broader sense, "disorder of the personality" is often used as equivalent to "mental illness" or "emotional illness:'

PERVERSION (SEXUAL PERVERSION)

A form of personality disorder, characterized by an alteration from the normal of the *aim* and/or the *object* of libidinal strivings. Examples: *sadism, masochism, voyeurism.*

PHANTASY

See fantasy.

PHOBIA

(1) An obsessive, unrealistic fear of an external object or situation. Some of the common phobias are *acrophobia,* fear of heights; *agoraphobia,* fear of open places; claustrophobia, fear of closed spaces; *mysophobia,* fear of dirt and germs; *xenophobia, fear* of *strangers.*

(2) The dread of an object, an act or a situation that is not realistically dangerous, but that has come to represent a danger.

Phobic, pertaining to phobias.

PHOBIC REACTION

One of the psychoneuroses, formerly called *anxiety hysteria,* characterized by the presence of phobias.

PRECONSCIOUS

One of the three levels of *awareness,* the quality attaching to an idea, a sensation or an emotion of which the subject is not spontaneously aware but can become aware with effort.

PREMORBID PERSONALITY

The status of an individual's personality (conflicts, defenses, strengths, weaknesses) before the onset of clinical illness.

PRIMARY GAIN

The adjustment (adaptational) value of a neurotic symptom per se.

PROJECTION

One of the *defense mechanisms,* a technic whereby feelings, wishes or attitudes, originating within the subject, are attributed by him to persons or other objects in his environment.

PROJECTIVE TESTS

(1) Psychological tests used as a diagnostic tool. Among the most common projective tests is the Rorschach (inkblot) test.

(2) A relatively unstructured, although standardized, psychological test in which the subject is called upon to respond with a minimum of intellectual restrictions, thereby revealing characteristic drives, defenses and attitudes. (Examples are the Rorschach and the Thematic Apperception Tests.)

PSYCHE
Actually synonymous with *mind;* frequently used in expressions suggesting a mind-body duality, as, for example, "psychosomatic," "psychophysiologic," and "psychic versus organic factors:'

PSYCHIATRY
That branch of medicine that deals with the causes, the diagnosis, the treatment and the prevention of mental disorders.

Psychiatrist, a physician specializing in psychiatry.

Psychiatric nurse, a nurse specializing in the care of patients having mental disorders.

Psychiatric team, a group of professional and semiprofessional persons working together under the direction of a psychiatrist in the treatment of psychiatric, patients. (Usually the membership of such a team includes psychiatrist, psychiatric nurse, clinical psychologist, psychiatric social worker, occupational therapist, and psychiatric aide.)

PSYCHOANALYSIS
(1) A theory of human development and behavior, a method of research, and a system of psychotherapy, originally described by Sigmund Freud (1856-1939). Through analysis of free associations and interpretation of dreams, emotions and behavior are traced to the influence of repressed instinctual drives in the unconscious. Psychoanalytic treatment seeks to eliminate or diminish the undesirable effects of unconscious conflicts by making the patient aware of their existence, origin, and inappropriate expression.

(2) The term designates 1. a *method* of (a) psychotherapy and (b) psychological research, and 2. a body of *facts and theories* of human psychology. Both the method and the body of knowledge represent the work of Sigmund Freud and his followers. *Psychoanalyst,* a professional person, usually a physician, who has received specialized formal training in the theory and the practice of psychoanalysis.

PSYCHONEUROSIS (NEUROSIS)
(1) One of the two major categories of emotional illness, the other being the psychoses. It is usually less severe than a psychosis, with minimal loss of contact with reality.

(2) A mild to moderately severe illness of the personality (mind), in which the ego function of reality-testing is not gravely impaired, and in which the maladjustment to life is of a relatively limited nature.

Psychoneurotic, pertaining to or characteristic of a psychoneurosis.

PSYCHOPATHIC PERSONALITY
An older term for one of the varieties of *personality disorder,* roughly synonymous with the current (official) category of "sociopathic personality disturbance," a form of illness characterized by emotional immaturity, the use of short-term values and behavior that is asocial or antisocial.

PSYCHOSIS
(1) A major mental disorder of organic and/or emotional origin in which there is a departure from normal patterns of thinking, feeling, and acting. Commonly characterized by loss of contact with reality, distortion of perception, regressive behavior and attitudes, diminished control of elementary impulses and desires, and delusions and hallucinations. Chronic and generalized personality deterioration may occur. A majority of patients in public mental hospitals are psychotic.

(2) A very serious illness of the personality (mind), involving a major impairment of ego function, particularly with respect to reality-testing, and revealed by signs of a grave maladjustment to life.

Psychotic, pertaining to or afflicted with psychosis.

PSYCHOSOMATIC
Adjective to denote the constant and inseparable interdependence of the psyche (mind) and

the soma (body). Most commonly used to refer to illnesses in which the manifestations are primarily physical with at least a partial emotional cause.

PSYCHOSURGERY
A form of neurosurgery in which specific tracts or other limited portions of the brain are severed or destroyed with the intention of producing favorable effects upon the patient's psychological status.

PSYCHOTHERAPY
(1) The term for any type of mental treatment that is based primarily upon verbal or nonverbal communication with the patient in distinction to the use of drugs, surgery, or physical measures such as electric or insulin shock.

(2) A term with many shades of meaning. In the broadest sense it is equivalent to "psychological treatment measures;" in a narrower sense *psychotherapy* refers to a direct relationship between one or more patients and a professional person, the therapist, in which the latter endeavors "to provide new life experiences which can influence the patient in the direction of health" (Levine).

PSYCHOTIC PERSONALITY
A variety of personality disorder, synonymous with the current official term "personality pattern disturbance," in which, despite the absence of the usual clinical symptoms of psychosis, the individual's fundamental conflicts and defenses are those of a *psychotic*.

R

RATIONALIZATION
The process of constructing plausible reasons for one's responses (usually to avoid awareness of neurotic motives).

REACTION FORMATION
One of the *defense mechanisms,* a technic whereby an original attitude or set of feelings is replaced in consciousness by the opposite attitude or feelings.

REALITY-TESTING
The process of determining objective (usually external) reality, a function of the ego.

RECONSTITUTE
To form again. The term is used of a personality that, having become more or less disorganized through illness, resumes its previous defense measures and type of adjustment.

REGRESSION
(1) The partial or symbolic return to more infantile patterns of reacting.
(2) One of the *defense mechanisms;* a process in which the personality retraces developmental steps, moving backward to earlier interests, defenses, and modes of gratification.

REPRESSION
(1) A defense mechanisms, operating unconsciously, that banishes unacceptable ideas, emotions, or impulses from consciousness or that keeps out of consciousness what has never been conscious.
(2) One of the *defense mechanisms,* a technic whereby thoughts, emotions and/or sensations are thrust out of consciousness.

REVERSAL
One of the *defense mechanisms,* a technic whereby an instinctual impulse is seemingly turned into its opposite, as, for example, when *sadism* is replaced by *masochism*.

S

SADISM

A form of perversion characterized by the experiencing of erotic pleasure in inflicting pain on another person. Often used more broadly as meaning the enjoyment of cruelty. *(See* Masochism.)

SCHIZOID

Schizophrenic-like. *Schizoid personality,* a form of *personality disorder* (subgroup of *psychotic personality)* characterized by withdrawn, self-centered, often eccentric behavior.

SCHIZOPHRENIA

(1) A severe emotional disorder of psychotic depth, characteristically marked by a retreat from reality with delusion formation, hallucinations, emotional disharmony, and regressive behavior. Formerly called dementia praecox. Its prognosis has improved in recent years.

(2) One of the major *functional psychoses;* more accurately, a group of interrelated symptom syndromes, having in common a number of features, including *associative looseness, autistic thinking, ambivalence* and inappropriateness of *affect*. The classic subgroups are: *catatonic, paranoid, simple* and *hebephrenic* schizophrenia; other varieties are: *schizoaffective, undifferentiated, childhood* and *latent* schizophrenia. *Schizophrenic,* pertaining to or afflicted with schizophrenia.

SECONDARY GAIN

The adjustment value or gratification that occurs as a result of the way in which a patient's environment responds to his illness (not an integral part of the symptoms per se).

SELF-CONCEPT

A person's image of himself, usually his conscious image.

SENILE

Pertaining to (extreme) old age, particularly to the deterioration in adjustment capacity occurring in old age.

Senile psychosis, an organic psychosis resulting from the brain damage accompanying advanced age.

SHOCK TREATMENT

A form of psychiatric treatment in which electric current, insulin, or carbon dioxide is administered to the patient and results in a convulsive reaction to alter favorably the course of mental illness.

SIMPLE SCHIZOPHRENIA

One of the four classic *schizophrenia* subgroups, characterized by slow, insidious onset and chronic course, with the illness being shown by emotional coldness, withdrawal and eccentricity, rather than by more striking symptoms.

SOMATOPSYCHIC

A term of recent coinage, intended to indicate psychological effects of somatic pathology.

SPLIT PERSONALITY

A term calling attention to the schizophrenic's inappropriate-ness of affect; the "split" is thus between emotions and ideation.

STRESS

Any circumstance that taxes the adjustment capacity of the individual.

SUBJECT

The person under discussion or study, as, for example, a patient or a person upon whom an experiment is performed.

SUBLIMATION

(1) A defense mechanism, operating unconsciously, by which instinctual but consciously unacceptable drives are diverted into personally and socially acceptable channels.

(2) One of the *defense mechanisms,* the only one that is never pathogenic; a technic whereby the original aim or *object* of a basic drive is altered in a manner that allows the release of tension and, at the same time, is socially acceptable.

SUPEREGO

One of the three major aspects or agencies of the mind; similar to the term "conscience" but more inclusive since it involves both conscious and unconscious components. (*See* Ego.)

SUPPRESSION

A technic of adjustment -- differing from the *defense mechanisms* in that it is fully conscious and very rarely pathogenic -- whereby the ego denies expression to a thought or an impulse. (It is often contrasted with *repression,* which is automatic, unconsciously effected and frequently pathogenic.)

SYMBOLISM

The use of one mental image to represent another.

T

TOXIC

Pertaining to, or due to the action of, a poison.

Toxic *psychosis,* a psychosis brought about by the action of a poisonous substance or, more broadly, a psychosis brought about by any chemical interference with normal metabolic processes (grouped with the *organic psychoses*).

TRANSFERENCE

The attributing by the subject, to a figure in his current environment, of characteristics first encountered in some figure of his early life, and the experiencing of desires, fears, and other attitudes toward the current figure that originated in the relationship with the past figure. The term is most commonly used with respect to feelings of a patient toward his therapist.

Counter-transference, transference feelings of a therapist toward his patient.

TRAUMA

Harm or injury; sometimes, the circumstances productive of harm or injury. In psychiatry, the term is inclusive of purely emotional as well as physical injury.

Traumatic, harmful, pertaining to trauma.

TRAUMATIC NEUROSIS (WAR NEUROSIS)

An acute morbid reaction related to *psychoneurosis* but occurring only in response to overwhelming trauma or stress. The condition is characterized by a temporary, partial disorganization of the personality, followed by such symptoms as anxiety, restlessness, irritability, impaired concentration, evidence of autonomic dysfunction and repetitive nightmares in which the traumatic experience is "relived."

TURNING AGAINST THE SELF

One of the *defense mechanisms,* a technic in which an unacceptable drive (usually aggressive) is diverted from its original object and (unconsciously) made to operate against the self, in whole or in part.

U

UNCONSCIOUS
(1) That part of the mind the content of which is only rarely subject to awareness. It is the repository for knowledge that has never been conscious or that may have been conscious briefly and was then repressed.
(2) In psychiatry, one of the three *levels* of *awareness;* thoughts, sensations, and emotions at this level cannot enter the subject's awareness through any voluntary effort on his part, but they continue to exert effects upon his behavior.

UNDOING
One of the *defense mechanisms,* a technic in which a specific action is performed that is (unconsciously) considered by the subject to be in some sense the opposite of a previous unacceptable action (or wish), and thus to neutralize ("undo") the original action.

V

VEGETATIVE SIGNS (OF DEPRESSION)
A traditionally grouped set of findings, including anorexia, weight loss, constipation, amenorrhea, insomnia and "morning-evening variation in mood," that, when found in combination, are indicative of severe depression.

VOYEURISM
A form of *personality disorder* (more specifically, of *perversion*), in which the subject receives his principal erotic gratification in clandestine peeping.

W

WAXY FLEXIBILITY
A phenomenon, associated with *catatonic schizophrenia,* in which the body, particularly the extremities, will remain for long periods of time in any positions selected by the examiner.

www.ingramcontent.com/pod-product-compliance
Lightning Source LLC
Chambersburg PA
CBHW081824300426
44116CB00014B/2473